The
Yellow Nib

The Yellow Nib is the annual journal of the Seamus Heaney Centre for Poetry at Queen's University Belfast. The title of the journal is inspired by a bird-call – or rather, by how that call inspired an anonymous Irish scribe of the ninth century to write the verses you see in the margin of this page. The aim of *The Yellow Nib* is simple: to publish good writing.

Int én bec
ro léc feit
do rinn guip
 glanbuidi

fo-ceird faíd
ós Loch Laíg,
lon do chraíb
 charnbuidi

9th century Irish

The small bird
chirp-chirruped:
yellow neb,
 a note-spurt.

Blackbird over
Lagan water.
Clumps of yellow
 whin-burst!

Seamus Heaney

the little bird
that whistled shrill
from the nib of
 its yellow bill:

a note let go
o'er Belfast Lough—
a blackbird from
 a yellow whin

Ciaran Carson

GENERAL EDITOR
Ciaran Carson

ADDRESS FOR CORRESPONDENCE
The Seamus Heaney Centre for Poetry
School of English
Queen's University Belfast
Belfast BT7 1NN

phone: +44 (028) 9097 1070
email: shc@qub.ac.uk
www.qub.ac.uk/heaneycentre

TRADE ORDERS AND DISTRIBUTION
Cormac Austin
Blackstaff Press
4c Heron Wharf
Sydenham Business Park
Belfast BT3 9LE

phone: +44 (028) 9045 5006
email: cormac.austin@blackstaffpress.com
www.blackstaffpress.com

ISBN 978-0-85640-813-7

The
Yellow Nib

The Literary Journal of the
Seamus Heaney Centre for Poetry

VOLUME 3

2007

This volume published in 2007 by
Blackstaff Press
4c Heron Wharf, Sydenham Business Park
Belfast BT3 9LE
with the assistance of the Arts Council of Northern Ireland

ARTS
COUNCIL
of Northern Ireland

Typeset by Carole Lynch, County Sligo, Ireland
Printed in England by Antony Rowe

A CIP catalogue record for this book
is available from the British Library

ISBN 978-0-85640-813-7

www.blackstaffpress.com

Contents

CONTENTS

Editorial

Thirteen Ways of Looking
at a Blackbird

I

Welcome to Blackbird Fashions. We believe it's important to know where your clothes come from. Whose hands made what you're wearing? Blackbird Fashions makes unique, handmade articles of clothing, accessories and toys for the modern girl and boy.

II

No reconnaissance aircraft in history has operated in more hostile airspace or with such complete impunity as the Lockheed SR-71 Blackbird. It is the fastest aircraft propelled by air-breathing engines. The Blackbird's performance and operational achievements place it at the pinnacle of aviation developments during the Cold War. It acquired the official name Blackbird for the special black paint that covered the airplane. This paint was formulated to absorb radar signals, to radiate some of the tremendous air-frame heat generated by air friction, and to camouflage the aircraft against the dark sky at high altitudes.

III

Described by the *New Yorker* as 'friendly, unpretentious, idealistic and highly skilled', *eighth blackbird* promises its ever-increasing audiences provocative and engaging performances. It is widely lauded for its performing style – often playing from memory with virtuosic and theatrical flair.

IV

Blackbird Café is the ever popular, funky ambient venue for all people – young or old – without pretension or boundaries. Blackbird Café is the definitive 'people's café'. Blackbird Café is situated on Level 1 of the Cockle Bay Wharf.

V

Blackbird Technologies Inc. offers the perfect combination of people, technology and experience to provide state-of-the-art technology-based solutions to intelligence, defense and corporate challenges. Every day, the Blackbird team applies its expertise to develop tools and capabilities critical to the successful prosecution of the global war on terrorism, to the information technology needs of the Intelligence and Defense Communities, and to similar challenges in the private sector. Please contact us for further information.

VI

Blackbird Designs carries a variety of products. We are most well known for our Blackbird Bikes and our Quadribent™ side-by-side recumbent quad bicycles. We offer many parts, accessories and adaptive equipment as well as options to customize vehicles.

VII

MICROSOFT SHOOTS DOWN BLACKBIRD – Microsoft Corp. has decided to abandon development work on the non-HyperText Markup Language version of Internet Studio, formerly known as Blackbird, on its online publishing tool.

VIII

Blackbird Boats are a new breed of boats. Designed with computer assistance, Blackbird Boats have set a new standard for blending the strength and aesthetic beauty of wood with the technology to make wooden boating a carefree experience. From the anti-fouling bottom paint to the high-tech wood finish, maintenance of all our mahogany boats leaves fiberglass boat owners envious.

IX

We founded Blackbird Architects in order to practise the highest quality and most sensitive design, using common sense and an economy of means. We strive to realize beautiful, elegant, and sustainable solutions in all our work. Our philosophy leads us to value radiant space and light over expensive materials and difficult details.

X

DINING AT BLACKBIRD

Dinner Appetizers

pinenut gazpacho with soppressata, apricot, spring radish and nasturtium; charcuterie plate with game bird terrine, 'corned duck', pickled ramps, fingerlings and soft boiled quail egg; west coast mussel soup with white fish, saffron, garlic and basil; salad of endives, crispy potatoes, basil, Dijon, pancetta and poached egg; capriole Kentucky tomme cheese salad with marinated white asparagus, spring radishes, sorrel, cucumber and hazelnut oil; crispy confit of swan creek farm suckling pig with sour cherries, roasted chioggia beets, housemade prosciutto and local cress; braised octopus with fresh shell beans, smoked paprika, zucchini bread and pluots.

We are located in West Loop Chicago at 619 W Randolph Street.

XI

The inactive Blackbird Mine lies 25 miles west of Salmon, Idaho, and some 13 miles south of the Salmon River. Mining operations starting in the late 1800s extracted gold, cobalt and copper ore from both underground and open-pit mines. Environmental concerns have been releases of cobalt, copper, iron and arsenic into Blackbird, South Fork of Big Deer, Big Deer and Panther Creeks. Early clean up collections collected contaminated run-off water in the mine area and treated it for copper and cobalt. They also stabilized waste-rock piles.

XII

The wait is over. Blackbird's second full-length album, *Bird's Eye View*, is now available on Alpha Pup Records. Produced by Paris Zax, the album features thirteen brand-new tracks. Scoop it from iTunes or the Alpha Pup Store.

XIII

I know noble accents
And lucid, inescapable rhythms;
But I know, too,
That the blackbird is involved
In what I know.

WALLACE STEVENS
'Thirteen Ways of Looking at a Blackbird'

CIARAN CARSON
AUGUST 2007

Three Poems

SINEAD MORRISSEY

Storm

It was already Gothic
enough, what with that
King-of-Versailles-size bed
with room for me and two
or three liveried footmen;

wall-lights like candle-
shafts in fake pearl and cut
glass; and the stranded
little girl in the photographs
growing sorrowful –

her cascade sleeves, her floral
crown – as though taken
by Lewis Carroll. All afternoon
the church bells rang out
their warning. Cumulostratus

ascended into heaven.
Evening and the white forked
parting of the sky fell
directly overhead, casements
rattled on hinges and Thunder

may as well have summoned
the raggle-taggle denizens
of his vociferous world:
the ghouls, the gashed, the dead
so bored by now of being

dead they flock to gawk –
sanctuary was still sanctuary
except more so, with the inside
holding flickeringly, and the
outside clamouring in.

A Device for Monitoring Brain Activity
by Shining Light into the Pupil

after Petr Borkovec

A liner in the foreground of the Lough
– dead-centre but already passing on –
white as a tent in Plantagenet France. I walked
the steep road to the shore, which tips
the earth into ocean,
levers ocean up to heaven,
as though broken in the middle by a hand.
I watched for gulls where the Threemilewater
empties and spills. The liner shone.

Ducks were tugging each other out to sea.
They rode each wave the liner sent
percussively. They wobbled and re-gathered
in the succeeding calm. Across the Lough,
– if only for a moment – hillsides
snided in gorse bushes crackled and sang.
A straggle of crows, backs to the enemy,
were guarding the bars fencing the cenotaph
while cormorants out on the platform,

huddled and avuncular and jet-dark
as obsidian, were as standing stones
to the wash beneath them: the tide
advanced, the water glistening.

Smashed mussel shells banked
against the sides of rocks burned blue
in the sun. And though the waves from the ship
still repeated along the bulwark, decreasing
in intensity, the door to the sea floor stood open
in between: sand, weeds, a trolley
taking several hundred years to disappear.
Light fell unequally at the horizon's vanishing-
point as though the edge of the world glared upwards.

The liner shone all the while.
Absorbing the sunlight, throwing it out again.
That shimmering, regal tent, I thought,
is almost like a ship: complete with passengers
and a captain's banquet. It could be that.
Brightness blurred the skin of everything.
I watched the gulls flare white
above the river mouth and saw, in hours,
how their wings, to a still-blue sky, would answer black.

Found Architecture

These days are all about waiting. What would you say
if I tried to explain how my single true activity
this wet and shivery May is 'found architecture'?

As the giver of an Italian kaleidoscope
that makes its heel–toe shapes, not from beads or seeds
or painted meticulous details, but from the room,

from whatever room I happen to be in,
or from the street, always eager and unerringly
democratic, you stand slightly to the south of me

with your head raised and I imagine you smiling.
The day it arrived I mangled the blue of the bathroom
with the pistachio green of my bedroom ceiling

and sat entranced: such symmetrical splicing
of everything, anything, to make of my waiting-house
a star-pointed frame that entered and left

itself behind as the cylinder turned. Any light that there was
was instantly mystical – a crack in the pattern's
typography, like the door at the end of the corridor

shedding radiance. Yesterday evening, by the sea,
a strangled sealed-off swamp by a walkway
threw up, suddenly, the Aboriginal outback:

rotted glands of a pond between knee-high grasses
and a white tree undoing itself in its ink-
stained surfaces. The tree looked like a crocodile's ribcage

as I passed along the perimeter, or the wide-
propped jawbone of a whale. Until it became, the further
I walked, a canoe, asleep on the water and fettered

with algae. Another dead branch sat up
in the grass like the head of an otter and talked.
This, too, was found architecture. And all the usual,

of course: skeletons of geranium leaves on window-
sills long afterwards; snake skins, clouds.
Beaches are full of it: found architecture being

the very business of beaches. Most recently
(and most disarmingly) this: handed to me in a roll
of four like mug-shot photographs from a machine,

his seahorse spine, his open-shut anemone
of a heart, and the row of unbelievable teeth
shining high in the crook of his skull as though back-

stitched into place. From blood and the body's
inconsolable hunger I have been my own kaleidoscope –
five winter-bleached girls on a diving board, ready to jump.

Two Poems

MARTIN MOONEY

The Ballad of Moscow Joe

In the war of words between Philomena
Begley and Susan McCann – who was who and which was queen
of Irish country music – I lost two figurine-

encrusted art-cars, torched by yobs with a grudge
against what's beautiful. That was the thick end of a wedge
that had seen my wife abandon our marriage

as well as the bungalow I glorified with collaged nick-
nacks, doctored garden ornaments, objets trouvés, hand-picked
junk, notices to the world in general and Carnlough

in particular. To her it was nothing but Merz,
to me it was – as she had been – a way of living with the world's
embarrassment of riches without it breaking our hearts.

Which are born broken: all this stuff, these assemblages
and amateur road-signs, is just the wages
of heartbreak, and when my children launch their purge

The Yellow Nib, Vol. 3, 2007, pp 7–11
© Martin Mooney

will all be swept away: as Philomena might well sing,
this ain't my home unless you wear my ring ...
So bulldoze the bungalow. All this furious decorating

was only ever meant to reconcile me to the lack
of ... Well, when country music's played in reverse on a tape deck,
your truck starts, your dog gets better, your girl comes back.

Banning Frankenstein
Belfast, 1932

1

A shipyard in the Ice Age. The slips are concrete
glaciers plunged in the Lough. You expect

the oily water to flash-freeze, or boil and rage,
but nothing happens. Cranes like laboratory

clamps or lightning-catchers bristle overhead
but the cloud is limp. Yes we have no bananas

no money no piano in the parlour but at least
there is no poverty under the blankets.

We make love to breed more idle hands,
of course we do. There is safety in numbers.

The indoor bathtub bathes a hoard of coal
while our children go barefoot and foul-mouthed

in the cinderbowls of last year's bonfires.
They flock to hear the mad scientists of the gospel

preach the Good News: if God had ever loved us,
He would have made us wealthy men, elsewhere.

2

Whose hand is this? When was it branded
D for Dieb? Why have I woken
in this town of smoke and open drains

whose citizens gather at churches and cold
manufactories angry at something
I seem to have done in a previous life.

Die Erbsünde. I have inherited the inner
organs of beggars, traitors, insolent apprentices.
My right eye is the brown eye of a heretic,

my left an atheist green. When I break free
of the crowd and make for the estuary,
I sink waist-deep in mud under the weight

Of the head on my shoulders, the burden
of other people's crimes. I drag my unhealed sutures
towards the slum liberties of Ballymacarrett

where the poor lever up pavers from the street
and pile them like dark apples, eggs
fresh from the furnace, and baked black.

3

'[He] shall not reveal any of his Master's Secrets, nor
conceal his loss or prejudice when known to him, but
shall in due time discover and do his utmost to prevent
the same. He shall not be guilty of drinking, nor
accessory to any riots or tumults on the street, nor haunt
idle or debauched company. He shall not walk in
processions. He shall not commit fornication, nor
contract Matrimony within the said Term ... but shall in
all respects promote his master's interests, and behave
and acquit himself as becomes a faithful and diligent
apprentice and shall during the whole Term aforesaid,
provide all the Tools and Implements necessary for
learning and practising his said Trade.'

– from the Harland and Wolff apprentice's oath

4

God's is the last word on the Police Committee
but He casts His vote by proxy. We

settle our rumps on maroon velour and feast
our eyes on the hand of dusty light,

the horror on the wall. A few minutes only
makes up our minds: we must spare the citizens

this insult to the brain, and Christ this garbled
version of the Word, this anti-resurrection.

While the unemployed riot, disdaining the work-
house, raging at the means test, we narrow

our eyes our eyes our eyes rather than pluck
them out. Mene mene tekel upharsin.

We padlock the picture house, but not before
we see the monster die, the screen darken,

and take this secret back to our villas
in Belmont and Strandtown, Malone, Stranmillis.

Life is a matter of electricity and original sin.
Is body-parts. Ye must be born again.

The Rainbow and the Frog
Modern Japanese Haiku

DAVID BURLEIGH

There are no blackbirds in Japan, though the frog has become emblematic of the haiku in much the same way that the blackbird has of early Irish lyric. Writing on 'Early Irish Nature Poetry', Seamus Heaney himself sees a parallel between 'Bashō's frog plopping into its pool in seventeenth-century Japan' and 'Belfast's blackbird clearing its throat over the lough almost a thousand years earlier'.[1] The number of syllables in the Irish poem is actually no greater than in Bashō's longest verse, while the whin blossom ties it to a season, as haiku usually demands. Bashō's imagery might even have included a yellow flower, had he followed the suggestion of one of his disciples, but then the poem would probably have been forgotten.

Two aspects of Bashō's frog piece mark its originality. One is that he refers to the 'sound of water', rather than the 'song' of the frog, as had become conventional by then. Frogs made their first appearance in Japanese poetry in an eighth-century anthology, and the aesthetics steadily developed through subsequent gatherings of verse. By Bashō's time it had become common to match the frog with a reference to kerria, a flowering shrub with blooms of buttercup-yellow. This was what his disciple had suggested, but Bashō rejected the idea, producing something more startling and new. There are now more than a hundred different English versions of this little poem.[2]

The Yellow Nib, Vol. 3, 2007, pp 12–23
© David Burleigh

The first translation into English by a native speaker was done by Lafcadio Hearn (1850–1904), the Greek-Irish-American commentator on Japan:

Old pond – frogs jumped in – sound of water.[3]

Two problems confronting the translator show up here. First, there is the matter of lineation, for the verse is written, albeit vertically, in a single line in Japanese (though it may be fragmented in calligraphy). And secondly there is the question of number, whether there is one frog or more than one. It is not true that there are no plurals in Japanese, but they are only used in certain cases. Since none is indicated here, there may just as well be several frogs as only one, leaving the reader free to imagine. But in English we must always choose, and so the 'early swallow' given below for a verse by a modern woman poet might also be a larger number.

What was perhaps the most widely circulated early version of the frog poem was given to the world by a man from Derry. W.G. Aston (1841–1911), who went out to Japan as a student interpreter attached to the British Legation, later wrote *A History of Japanese Literature* (1899), the first book on this subject in a Western language, and for many years the only one. Aston renders the seventeen syllables in three lines, to represent the pattern of three phrases:

An ancient pond!
With a sound from the water
Of the frog as it plunges in.[4]

The three-line format has now become more or less standard, though little attempt is usually made to preserve the 5-7-5-syllable pattern of the original. It is argued that the meaning can be represented in fewer syllables in English, and that any more is padding. This is not invariably true, but has an element of truth. In my own attempts to render modern haiku, I often try to achieve the syllabic pattern, to give the piece some kind of shape, but am prepared to abandon it if it simply doesn't work.

The other effect that Aston reveals is the temptation to reverse the order of the contents into something that sounds more natural in English syntax. This is a problem that the brevity of haiku sometimes makes acute, and must be worked against. It is necessary, at the same time, to try and create something that can be read with pleasure, otherwise the whole exercise is pointless. Some people think that translations ought to sound a little strange, to remind the reader that the poem is from another language, but a literal rendering will not always take us very far. That said, however, there have been some remarkable translations done that endeavour to preserve the unpunctuated simplicity and directness of haiku in Japanese.

A unique part of the haiku aesthetic is its use of 'cutting' or division somewhere within the poem, and often a special word is used for this. After the 'old pond' in Bashō's verse, there is the exclamation *ya*, a word with no translatable meaning, the purpose of which is only to create a pause. Such terms can best be represented by punctuation marks in English, such as an exclamation mark or a dash or a colon, though it is difficult sometimes to decide which one is appropriate. Abandoning punctuation altogether, as some do, muddles the meaning, so that we are then unsure which nouns and verbs should go together. Dangling participles are likewise a hazard. For myself, I prefer to use dividing marks. For the selection here, I have chosen verses that seemed to go comfortably into the syllabic pattern of 5-7-5.

Bashō's greatest rival for popular attention these days is a poet called Taneda Santōka (1882–1940), who submerged the unhappiness of his personal life by drinking heavily and writing haiku:

A wintry drizzle –
into the drizzly mountains
setting off on foot.[5]

Like Bashō, he wandered the country dressed in the garb of a Buddhist priest, and the late autumn rainfall that he mentions was much admired by Bashō. But there the resemblances end, for, although this is a regular verse, Santōka was primarily a free-form poet, whose work developed out of an experimental strand in haiku in the early part of the last century. The enduring mode, among the many who still compose today, is overwhelmingly regular in form.

The selection of modern haiku given below is taken, though not exclusively, from a new anthology compiled by the Modern Haiku Association, an organisation set up after World War Two.[6] The first two verses are by older poets, both male, and in each case the poem is well known. The second of them points up another problem in translation, for in English it is considered better style to avoid word-for-word repetition, and so I have varied the phrasing a little. It is often impossible, as becomes evident in some examples later, to avoid enjambement, ending one of the lines with an article or preposition. The poets' names are given in Japanese order, family name first, and some of them are invented poetic names. All those that end in 'ko' belong to female poets. The order of presentation is chronological, from the beginning of the twentieth century.

Some allusions in the poems need a little explanation. Original haiku in English, particularly in the United States, scarcely ever allude to literature in English, yet in Japanese they sometimes do so. It is by no means unusual to find that Itami Kimiko incorporates a line from William Blake. Reference to the month of August, in post-war haiku, usually invokes the dropping of the atomic bomb on Hiroshima, and this certainly informs the verse by Kuroda Momoko. There is a suggestion in another verse, by Ishi Kanta, of the well-known story of 'The Bamboo-Cutter's Daughter', about an extraterrestrial princess who finally returns to her home on the moon. The first phrase used by Fuyuno Niji is exactly the same as the opening of a famous verse by Bashō, about looking over the rough sea towards the island of Sado, and inevitably recalls this. Such references are common, and contribute to what the American scholar Haruo Shirane describes as the participation of every haiku poet in creating the One Great Poem, which is formed out of an endlessly growing body of allusions.[7] The poet's name, 'Niji', means 'rainbow', which is the subject of another poem.

Takahara Kōji's verse is arranged a little differently because the original has deliberate gaps. There have been some experiments with the format of haiku in modern times, the most famous of which, by Takayanagi Jūshin (1923–1983), is also a verse about a rainbow:

> Where it arches over backwards
> a rainbow   at its peak:
>
> the gallows.

But what is more interesting is the subject itself. There are very few classical references to rainbows in Japanese literature, and it did not become a season-word until modern times. Since the 1920s it has been recognised as a reference to summer. I find it odd myself that such a clear and mysterious natural phenomenon, despite having nothing to do with pots of gold or lemon drops, should only have joined the poetic vocabulary so recently.

The *hai* of haiku means 'play', and some of the poems are obviously frivolous, while others have a grimmer message. Some modern haiku make no reference to nature or the season, and this may be the case with the verse by Yotsuya Ryū, in which the young widower is almost certainly remembering his late wife. The colour is given in the dictionary as 'light-crimson' or 'pink', but I have chosen 'rosy' for its sound. The last verse, by a popular young woman poet, offers a fresh take on a traditional image.

YAMAGUCHI SEISHI
1901–1994

A summer river …
the end of a rusty chain
soaks in the water.

KATŌ SHŪSON
1905–1993

The leaves will never
cease to fall: do not make haste,
don't ever hasten!

HOSOMI AYAKO
1909–1997

In my usual clothes
and my usual state of mind –
the blossoming peach.

NOMURA TOSHIRŌ
1911–2001

Solitary spring –
throwing a javelin and then
walking up to it.

IIJIMA HARUKO

1920–2000

Down on the bottom
of the fountain lies a spoon –
the summer has gone.

AKAO TŌSHI

1925–1981

Utterly different
from so many other things:
lace-cap hydrangea.

ITAMI KIMIKO

1925–

Hold infinity
right in the palm of your hand?
A garden of quince.

SUZUKI ISHIO

1925–

As if they were made
for looking up at mountains:
the eyes of a plaice.

KATŌ IKUYA
1929–

It's my destiny
to grow old with poetry –
the autumn nightfall.

TANIYAMA KAEN
1932–

Onto the war dead
the flies have already flown …
the flies multiply.

ORIGASA BISHŪ
1934–

To the brilliant field …
surely you can get a ride
on a butterfly?

TAKEDA SHIN'ICHI
1935–

Life and death of man:
a battle fought by chickens
in paddy stubble!

KURODA MOMOKO
1938–

Enormous haiku
must be dedicated in
the month of August.

FUYUNO NIJI
1943–2002

Rough waves on the sea –
inside the skipping rope it's
completely empty.

ISHI KANTA
1943–

I would leave the child
sat lightly on my shoulders
in care of the moon.

TSUBOUCHI NENTEN
1944–

Cherry blossom falls –
you too must turn into a
hippopotamus!

TAKAHARA KŌJI

1949–

The rainbow itself
    is burnt out by a rainbow …

the mind and the heart.

IMAI SEI

1950–

In the stadium
are ten thousand empty seats –
an early swallow.

TSUKUSHI BANSEI

1950–

Neither have I seen
nor have I ever been to
Utsunomiya.

ŌNISHI JUNJI

1954–

When the sugar bowl
falls over, the Milky Way
comes into being.

ISHIDA KYOKO
1958–

The immovable,
single point that is myself –
a gust of green leaves.

YOTSUYA RYŪ
1958–

Myself and yourself:
everything has been frozen
to a rosy hue.

SAKAITANI MASATO
1963–

Autumn butterfly
enters the maze of the sky
never to return.

AYUZUMI MADOKA
1965–

The prows of the ships
all point toward Mount Fuji:
first sight of the year.

ENDNOTES

1   An earlier English version of the blackbird poem 'Int én bec' can be found in
     Seamus Heaney's essay 'The God in the Tree: Early Irish Nature Poetry' in
     Preoccupations: Selected Prose: 1968–1978 (London: Faber, 1980).

2   For further versions, see Chapter 7 of Hiroaki Sato, *One Hundred Frogs: From Renga
     to Haiku in English* (New York & Tokyo: Weatherhill, 1983). The very first English
     translation was made by the haiku poet and reformer Masaoka Shiki (1867–1902).

3   This comes from the chapter on 'Frogs' in Lafcadio Hearn, *Exotics and Retrospectives*
     (Boston: Little, Brown, 1898).

4   Aston devotes several pages of his study to the poet, though he calls him 'Matsura
     [*sic*, instead of Matsuo] Bashō'. See Chapter IV of 'Book the Sixth' in *A History of
     Japanese Literature* (Yokohama: Kelly & Walsh / London: Heinemann, 1899).

5   This is the opening verse of a bilingual anthology of some five hundred modern
     haiku, by approximately 270 poets, due for publication in 2007, from which all but
     one of the subsequent verses have been drawn. The title of the book has not yet
     been announced.

6   Selections for this anthology have been made by members of the Modern Haiku
     Association (Gendai Haiku Kyōkai) in Japan, and the book will be published under
     its auspices. The English translations were initially prepared by various hands, and
     then revised by David Burleigh. Only the verse by Takayanagi Jūshin has been
     taken from another anthology, *A Hidden Pond* (Tokyo: Kadokawa, 1997), co-
     translated by Kōko Katō and David Burleigh; the poems by Hosomi Ayako, Nomura
     Toshirō and Iijima Haruko appear in both volumes. In several cases the wording has
     been further adjusted for the purpose of this article.

7   See, for example, Haruo Shirane, *Traces of Dreams: Landscape, Cultural Memory and
     the Poetry of Bashō* (Stanford: Stanford University Press, 1998).

Seventeen Haiku

FRANK ORMSBY

The field full of snow
so much a field full of snow
it needs a blackbird.

Tonight, in the smokeless zone, the drift
of fresh turf-smoke –
a Christmas gift!

Hares on the grass patch
between the runways. Ears flat.
Ready for take-off.

Lost among your wet things
on the kitchen floor,
those two raindrop earrings.

The Yellow Nib, Vol. 3, 2007, pp 24–26
© Frank Ormsby

Kneeling, we fill two buckets
to the brim. The well-
level does not change.

Sensing a haiku
opportunity – those two
blackbirds, right on cue!

The boiler growls in its out-
house. Winter gales
run wild on the mountain.

On the yard wall,
suddenly, a hooded crow.
Hard bastard. You can tell.

How relaxed she is,
that stray heifer,
shitting her way through the graveyard.

Missing the fish's jump,
we have to make do
with the splash and its ripples.

Swept out as worthless,
the curled, perfect shavings
from the carpenter's bench.

Above, the helicopter. Below,
in the restless streets,
its shadow.

Pity to disturb him –
moth on the bedroom curtains,
sleeping alone.

Cold as the Pole Star
the gush from the garden tap –
winter on my hands.

Mud from my father's grave.
A whole week now, father,
since I cleaned my shoes.

Breathe on the bus window.
Wipe it clear. The world
as it is without you.

At last the Ice Age recedes.
In our garden, heels-up,
a dead blackbird.

Guitar Man
Reflections on Davy Graham

TOBY LITT

I've been giving up guitar since the age of eleven and a half – because I couldn't play like John Williams on CBS *Records Presents John Williams* or Dave Gilmour on *Wish You Were Here* or Django Reinhardt on anything he recorded or, for the past year, because I can't play like Davy Graham on the CD reissue of *Folk, Blues and Beyond* (1964).

The most famous song on this album is 'Angi'.[1] It has been covered by a million bedroom guitarists, and also by Davy Graham's contemporaries, Bert Jansch (as 'Angie') and Paul Simon (as 'Anji'). And I'd like to write here about not being able to play 'Angi' (or 'Angie' or 'Anji').

It starts as casually as any recorded sound I know. The first notes, not as fully fretted as the later ones, are merely an out-breath – and the listener, travelling imaginatively back in time to the moment before the tape started rolling, knows there was an in-breath and an out-breath before that. In fact, what is implied, by these few seconds of chime, is a whole casual-disciplined existence – Davy Graham's existence.

After strolling in so lightly, 'Angi' continues for four foursquare bars. During this introduction, it has already achieved an unprecedented balance; it is absolutely rigid and, at the same time, it is flowing. This is an impossible architecture of molten steel. (The strings of Davy Graham's Gibson guitar would have been made of steel, although the three bass ones might have been copperwound.)

The Yellow Nib, Vol. 3, 2007, pp 27–33
© Toby Litt

What has been established, on the most basic level, during these thirteen seconds, is the thing that always separates competent musicians from incompetent: the ability to accompany oneself – to play two lines at once.

On the BBC TV documentary *Folk Britannia*, Graham mentioned how he tried for ten years to learn the Arab lute, the oud, but never quite mastered the 'question and answer, antiphonal responses between treble and bass'. That may be true. But there is definitely a dialogue going on here.

The bassline of 'Angi' is a very simple descending figure, and Davy Graham's statement of it is brutally direct. You'll be familiar with the plonk-plonk-kerplonk-plonk from some of its later incarnations. It's there, doubled up, as the first hook of the Kinks' 'Sunny Afternoon'. It's the basis of 'Stray Cat Strut' by the Stray Cats – which took 'Angi' across into a world of cartoon rockabilly. (Hard not to imagine T.C. growling it out to Officer Dibble.) Madness played around with it on the chorus of 'It Must Be Love', taking it down to the deadness of the bottom note, and then resurrecting it with duh-duhhr! The Cure jazzed it up for 'The Lovecats'. I can even hear it lurking around behind Britney Spears's 'Toxic'.

Where it came from, in the first place, is probably some unrecorded jazz jam. Somehow, it seems as eternal as the three-chord climb of 'La Bamba' (in fact, now I think of it, it's pretty close to 'La Bamba' played backwards). Wikipedia, however, credits Percy Mayfield's 'Hit the Road, Jack'. But maybe you could go further back, a lot further, and discover it buried in the 'Liebestod' of *Tristan und Isolde*.

Plonk-plonk-kerplonk-plonk. Why is this riff so popular? Partly because it sounds so utterly right, and partly because, when you pick up a guitar, the opening notes to 'Angi' will fall under your fingers. In *Revolution in the Head*, Ian MacDonald observes how John Lennon's style of composition was very much dependent on his 'lazy proclivity for finding sequences by moving his fingers as little as possible'.[2] Songs like 'Rain', 'Nowhere Man' and 'I'm So Tired' enact their semi-stasis on the guitar neck, where they came into existence, basing themselves around minimal movements – a C-chord to an F, a hammer-on, a note missed out. This laziness doesn't hold for 'Angi', or not for long, because, as soon as he's set up the attainable, Davy Graham begins to mess with your sense of the finger-possible.

As a basic rule, the thicker your guitar strings (technically, the heavier their gauge), the harder they will be to play, and the purer, more ringingly, they will sound. Nick Drake has a reputation for effeteness. But, going by his dexterity on 'Three Hours' or 'Time Has Told Me' or 'Road', he could easily have crushed your skull with his left hand. Thicker guitar strings vibrate more powerfully, so, in order to get a clean note out of them, you have to press them down harder on the fretboard. Harder still than this is to bend the strings, and keep the note ringing out rather than fuzzing up. In the second four bars of 'Angi', Davy Graham pulls off something that, to a non-guitarist, doesn't sound like much: he begins to bend lead-line notes on top of his downwardly clumping bass. What the guitarist knows, and marvels at, and is terrified by, is that Graham's left hand is at the bottom of the guitar's neck (though there's actually a capo involved, moving all this action up to the fourth fret). Here, on the first three frets, is where most strumming-type guitarists (out of Dylan by Young) play their tunes. If they ever attempt to bend a note, they will move their hands halfway up the neck – where it is much, much easier to push the string far enough to bend the note a tone or semi-tone. Graham bends notes which he shouldn't be able to bend, at least not with such insulting ease. To a guitarist, these second four bars say one thing: 'Fuck off – I'm better than you are.'

Behind most if not all twentieth-century note-bending is Louis Armstrong. And Davy Graham's syncopated slurs in 'Angi' are a years-later tribute to the kind of sliding soundworld Armstrong invented in 'West End Blues' and other epochal sides. This is the *Blues* part of *Folk, Blues and Beyond*, though it might as accurately have been *Folk, Jazz* . . . The pleasure in jazz is rarely in the centre of the notes but on their fraying margins. Think of the sad crack in Miles Davis's tone, or the sanctified hoarseness of John Coltrane, or even the going-out-of-tune boom of Thelonious Monk's straight-finger-struck piano. The tone of a guitar string changes when notes are played bent. That's why Jimi Hendrix sounds as he does – so many of his notes are struck when the string is stretched, two, three, four notes higher than if the string were just fretted. 'Voodoo Child

(Slight Return)' – or, if not bent up one or two notes, they are played
with vibrato, the rapid bending of the string. (Eric Clapton learnt to
do this – or learnt to avoid not doing this. Play your guitar too
straight and everything starts sounding like 'Greensleeves'. The blues
always goes at notes sideways.) Hendrix's playing becomes
increasingly more anguished. This is what most lead guitarists do:
push your fingers up to make the string tighter, it cries; let it loose
from this position, it sobs.

What is even more astonishing about Graham's playing is that the
notes underlying the bent note remain unaffected. As you bend a
string, it gets closer to the string beside it – and, simultaneously,
harder to keep that note held decently down. But you'll never hear a
badly sounded note on *Folk, Blues and Beyond*. Graham sounds like
he's playing Plato's guitar.

After this piece of disguised virtuosity, a coded message to all
guitarists listening, Graham returns to another three very straight
bars of his opening theme – though he finishes these off with a bluesy
solo on the higher strings. He's beginning to play with the constraints
of the form. The regularity of the bass-pulse continues, though. If this
were electronic music, it would be called 'motorik'. The discipline
involved is inexpressible. This is Man Machine Music.

But, to a guitarist of my level or above, 'Angi' seems just about do-
able. The opening downward plod holds out the hope that you
might, after a couple of weeks' practice, be able to cobble together
your own version of this tune. In the 1960s, you didn't exist as a folk
guitarist until you were able to play 'Angi'. It was your ticket into the
session, onto the stage; it was your introduction to young ladies with
long hair and atrociously thick knitwear. In order to do this, to get
your version, you would have to jettison all but the basic structure of
the song. Those high-up solo flourishes, they would be first to go.
What you'd be left with is a dogged bash through something
recognisable. In other words, a travesty.

'Angi' is still a rite of passage. Just type it in to YouTube and you'll
find several dozen virtuosi having a go.

None of them even comes close to Davy Graham. With every one,
you can tell that they are playing the tune just to prove that they can
play the tune. Their eyes fix on their hands, willing them not to make

a mistake. And almost all of them take it too fast – as if, simply by speeding things up, they could show they were better than Graham.

The versions by Bert Jansch and Paul Simon are both painful, in different ways. Jansch *wants* to sound rougher than Graham. His rhythm isn't as secure. Graham is an immaculate troubadour – someone fit to appear before the ladies of the court; Jansch is his Boho cousin, entertaining the marketplace. Paul Simon just wants to show that he's a good enough guitarist to get from one end of the damn thing to the other. There is no musicality on display, just the kind of sleepwalking fingering that comes from months of repetition. It constantly pushes to speed up. The end isn't a fulfilment, it's the finishing line; and the relief in the final jazzy chord is wince-making. Did it! No, you didn't.

And here is where I'd like to bring in another song from the reissue of *Folk, Blues and Beyond*. It is Graham's transcendent version of 'She Moved through the Fair'. To amateur guitarists like myself, this tune is a lot kinder than 'Angi', because it puts us out of our misery almost immediately. From the very first notes, it is clear that Graham's guitar is tuned in some weird modal way that would take you months to figure out. Then he's playing an entirely idiosyncratic mix of Celtic air, Delta blues, Indian raga, Moroccan trance music and Bluegrass fingerstyle. This is very much the *Beyond* of *Folk, Blues and Beyond*. And what it is beyond is everything. Here is O'Carolan jamming with the muezzin. Here is a musician as at home in the souk as in County Down. Davy Graham becomes a one-man Afro Celt Sound System. This is where the sitar on 'Paint it Black' comes from. But play Brian Jones's one-string twangings after Graham's spangle-making and you know who was the real genius. Similarly with the Beatles' 'Within You Without You' and the Kinks' 'See My Friends'. Jimmy Page's rip-offs of Davy Graham ('No "Stairway". Denied!') are rightly notorious.

With Davy Graham's 'She Moved through the Fair', the guitarist is left no choice – either you play it exactly as he did, note for note, which would be an exercise in imitative virtuosity, or you give up completely, accepting that your only way to challenge Graham would be to come up with a guitar style as innovative, achieved and sublime. And that is impossible. Graham's playing is imperialistic –

it is the pink on the map of World Music. He is a Rough Guide to
the strength of strings. You want to go exploring? Find some obscure
place no one's ever been. Well, Davy's lived there for three months.
He can show you the best bars, the best brothels, and the best
temples also.

Where 'Angi' makes me pick the guitar up again, 'She Moved
through the Fair' makes me abandon it. I will never achieve anything
like this in music. Far better for me to try and do it in words.

One thing remains puzzling. 'Angi' was supposedly written in
tribute to Davy Graham's girlfriend. But as a portrait of a young
woman with a bohemianly spelt name (Davy himself now insists on
'Davey'), 'Angi' is a complete failure. Nothing built of flesh and
blood ever sounded like this. Try to imagine her moving at this pace:
it's too fast for a walk and too slow for a run; it's too regular and
breathless even for a dance.

The clue comes in the next song on the album: 'Davy's Train
Blues'. 'Angi' can only be a locomotive – an American locomotive –
ambling through a Midwestern town; neither speeding up nor
slowing down, just implacably, imperturbably continuing on its way.
Only a mythic wreck would stop it ('The Wreck of the Old 97').
'Angi' travels in a straight line, on tracks, and wherever it is headed
isn't all that different to the place it's come from. There is variety,
along the way, but no climaxes; vistas open out, briefly, then are
curtailed. It's what's going on in the carriages that is full of life.

Harmonica players have always loved to imitate midnight
expresses: chuffing, moaning. Woody Guthrie did it, Bob Dylan also.
Here, Davy Graham manages it too. That plonk-plonk-kerplonk-
plonk is the regular rhythm of the wheels on the sleepers; the
maintained chime of the middle notes is the drone of the engine;
those bent upper notes are the trademark whoo-whoo-whoo riff of
the whistle. But this, to complicate things more, is an American
locomotive as heard by a European.

In his diary entry of 31 July 1917, Franz Kafka wrote: 'Sit on a
train, forget the fact, and live as if you were at home; but suddenly
recollect where you are, feel the onward-rushing power of the train,
change into a traveller, take a cap out of your bag, meet your fellow
travellers with a more sovereign freedom, with more insistence, let

yourself be carried towards your destination by no effort of your own, enjoy it like a child, become a darling of the women, feel the perpetual attraction of the window, always have at least one hand extended on the window sill.'[3]

ENDNOTES
1   Originally, 'Angi' was not on the album, but appeared on a separate EP called *3/4 A.D.*..
2   Ian MacDonald, *Revolution in the Head: The Beatles' Records and the Sixties* (London: Pimlico, 1998) p. 333.
3   Franz Kafka, *The Diaries of Franz Kafka, 1910–1923* (London: Penguin Modern Classics, 1972)

Seven Poems

ANDREW ELLIOTT

Breathless

Amy flings open the window and takes in two big lungfuls of
   Berlinerluft.
She hasn't been in Berlin so much as a day but already she can
   smell revolution
Like she used to smell bacon in Boston, exciting, forbidden,
   beginning to burn,
Blackening the edges of everything, buildings, windows, faces, eyes,
   the sun

And such ideas as she has hitherto held to be true – not bad ideas
   but ideas
Which Sabrina would scoff at if she weren't at that moment
   preoccupied
In a room across the street from Amy's, lying on her back, tossing
   off a cock
Like a bottle of schnapps from which she's attempting to extract
   the last drop.

How two such girls – despite the iron tram track between them –
   got to meet
Is a story I had hoped to tell here and so pre-empt my readers with
   rifles

From adopting positions on rooftops, in doorways, even astride
    equestrian monuments,
And preparing to take the gratuitous pot shots that will have me
    running for cover

Down streets already being criss-crossed by people holding on to
    their hats, hats
After all being important, though I don't have one myself, so I pop
    into a good haberdasher I know
Where the nice young man is happy to help and one leaves feeling
    quite the dandy,
Only to be brought up short by one's readers, beneath their banners
    browed and fisted.

Friends! Comrades! I begin. I could as easily just stood there and
    asked myself, '. . .?'
Like a man who's been painted into a corner might stare at the
    brush in his own hand.
Instead I juke back in. My young man has held out his hand and I
    take it
And together we run, my young man and I, until behind a door
    marked PRIVATE,

Where we have stopped to catch our breaths, he scribbles on the
    back of my hat's receipt,
Which – now he tells me! – I'd forgotten, the address of a teahouse
    he knows . . .
When I get back to Amy's room a bullet meant for me has hit the
    dressing table mirror
And the sun from between two buildings burns like a spider at the
    centre of its web.

Great Beauty

Amy is not a great beauty – lipless, hipless, I could go on –
But her red hair is to the wind what the word wind
Is to the mind of a woman like Sabrina who can remember
The red flags flying from the guns of the ships in Kiel harbour

And who would later take the train to Berlin in time to see
Karl Liebknecht proclaim from a balcony of the Kaiser's castle
A Socialist Republic of Germany and an east wind bring
To the twilight, snow like a message from the party in Moscow

That Sabrina should pass herself off as a boy and find herself
Rising on a steep learning curve at whose pinnacle her heart
Was to glow like a star and then come falling back to earth,
A cold black lump of nothing, waiting in its line for a trolley bus

But preserving at its centre an ember, which flares as she stares
Across the *Strasse* to where Amy is waiting in the opposite direction –
Berlin like a strongman, having brought them so close, preparing
To part them like a chest expander – when suddenly the wind

Blows Amy over – as gusts do do to all such tall untethered things –
And Sabrina to the wind entrusts her caution. *I'm a doctor!*
She shouts, *Let me through!* It fools no one, but people
Being people always like an excuse to participate from a distance

By gawping. *Hail a cab,* shouts Sabrina, cradling Amy, who's a little
Concussed. A cab in its own good time pulls up and Sabrina asks,
Where do you live? Amy, weirdly, can't remember so Sabrina
Says, *I'll take you to my place* ... She shouts an address in Wedding

And the driver, like a Dobermann pinscher, would have sniffed at it
Over his shoulder if Sabrina hadn't snapped, *And where the hell
Are you from, driver, Dalldorf?* Had I been that driver I'd have driven
Like the wind drives all before it with an eye on the rearview mirror.

The Meals of the Day

Breakfast

Sabrina wakes up in a mood so black that even a cup
Of black coffee can't lift it. When Amy refuses
To bring her another she lies there twisting her pubic hair
Like the handlebar moustaches of a well-waxed general.

Morning Break

A cup of green tea in a glass? A slice of watermelon
When in season? Not for Amy the bars of black chocolate
Whose foil she'll find between the sheets, irreducibly
Wrinkled and golden like the faeces of some mythical beast.

Lunch

Sabrina skips lunch like a heart skips a beat
And it leaves her feeling weak in her heart a little later
Like the beat her heart skipped is a beat skipped for ever.
I should be beaten on the bottom with a stick, she thinks.

Afternoon Break

A porcelain pot of darjeeling? A scone with jam and cream?
No. A pretzel, a Pepsi, taken on the hoof, or an apple
If she's on a health jag . . . The traffic lights changing from red
To green. A park bench, certainly. But in fall or in spring?

Dinner

Sabrina is almost always late. Amy prepares it alone
But rinsing a zucchini like a man masturbating only fills her
Full of sadness, so much seed going to waste for the want of
        a cunt.
Where the hell is she? thinks Amy, chopping it up into chunks.

Supper

Having put new black sheets on the bed, Amy takes off
All her clothes and spreads herself into the corners
Like marmalade. *Oh*, thinks Sabrina, annoyed,
It's going to take me hours to lick every inch of her off.

Paper Work

One can't imagine what thoughts were going through Amy's mind
As she lay like a long white scroll of paper, a small black stone
At every corner, but still, one has to try, it's my job after all
And – though I'd prefer to show my wife a wage I could be
    proud of –

Somebody's got to do it and I like to think that I've done it so far
Without too much complaint. It's not, it's true, the shortest straw
Though what a shorter straw might look like I'm not exactly
    certain …
I wouldn't want to work in a pet shop, pet shops give me the creeps.

The point I'm trying to make is this: while most men hold down
Decent jobs, pay substantial sums in taxes, have wives whose eyes
Light up at jewellery, my lot in life is not so easy yet I try not to
    take it
Personally when I announce, to all and sundry, the nature of
    my work

For I do announce it and if I feel myself being spurned I have
    no qualms
In saying what I've said once already here, that someone's got to do it
And, to be fair, most folks see the sense in that and I take the issue
No further. A man at the end of the day is a man and should –
    Goddamit! –

Be proud of himself except, of course, if he's a pedo or a murderer
In which case – *au contraire!* – he should be ashamed of himself. Me?
I'd lock 'em all in cages, take the keys, hire a boat and, using
    GPS, sail
Till I sat plumb atop the Mariana Trench, where it'd give me
    great delight

To pick each key by the tail and . . . whoa, I need to wind up here.
   Let's think ...
The small volcanic breasts I long assumed extinct, snow capped like two
Mount Fujis ...? I like it and I find it appropriate that a mind as fine
As Amy's is should be so tenderly transported, courtesy of
   lofty thoughts.

Three Road Movies

Distance

I feel like I'm the only child who long ago lost interest, in
     his parents
And where they were taking him, a future they claimed
They could see, through the windshield kept clear by the wipers,
Lashing left then right, like an argument to which there's no
     end in sight,

And who now prefers to kneel on the backseat of their Trabant P50
And stare through the blur of its volatile engine at the driver
(And her red-haired companion) of a slightly more powerful P60
A consistent, safe distance behind since we all left home that
     morning.

Damage

On the edge of a New Mexican mesa I was sitting, shoulder
     to shoulder,
With a woman I'd met in Las Cruces. We'd watched the sun set
     like a movie
And now that the desert below us was dark what remained of the
     highway
Off which we had turned was a red and white striped strip of light

Like two tectonic plates were sliding slowly past each other.
     I'd slipped
My arm around her waist. Our lives had been nothing to write
     home about.
Only God knew how we'd got there. When the force that drove
Our dusty lips to touch proved irresistible, did He flinch? Did He
     look away?

Destination

The car was large, black, but as it travelled west across the
   dustbowl state,
The sun on its roof, sunny side up, where should've been belongings
Or a chicken coop – *Gas station left behind it for dead? Ahead lie*
Another gas station? Is it their word against the word in the wires

That they're racing? – I saw it slowly elongate as the post-war boom
In speed kicked in … Shotgun on the spare chair like a sign
   pointing,
Thataway! I have seen their black car stretch horizon to horizon
Though it's gotten so fast it takes all day to go past and on into the
   night-time.

Havana

I was tunnelling under the Great Wall Of China
When who did I meet, tunnelling out,
But a lady I'd last seen in Havana, doing the salsa
At three in the morning when the building
We were dancing in collapsed; they do in Havana.

We were shy to begin with, a little bit frightened –
It was dark after all and we didn't have a candle.
She whispered, I sniffed; her breath smelt rooty.
When our noses accidently touched she said, *Great fortune* . . .
And I found I could tell that she was blushing

So I blushed too like it was some kind of flu
That it would've been impolite of me not to have caught.
Like two suns cancelling out each other, we kissed
And had a little think then we agreed to kiss again
Until not only were we kissing, despite our lips

Being muddy, we were kissing *because* our lips
Were muddy and when we felt a worm wriggling
In the mud of our mouths we didn't think to stop and wonder,
Much less to spit it out, for in the apple of our eye
That worm was the loveliest worm in the world

And we could not have been more happy – my tunnel
Was hers and hers was mine! – sucking back and forth
Like a noodle/spaghetti. Still, perhaps I sucked
Too hard or she did. Perhaps we'd stuff we'd left unsaid.
I had a little sleep – it's not unnatural – and when I woke up

My lady was gone. The tunnel she'd dug went on before me.
Someday there'll be light at the end of it. To her family
I'll come as consolation, I hope, though of my own
I can't be certain. I'd hate to be her, blinking up
At them all, holding their noses at her strong pong.

Still, we all pong one way or another in the end
And when they stoop to pull her out they will notice
How big her biceps have got though her legs will be weak,
Hairy like roots. Perhaps a wheelchair will be brought.
Two wheelchairs at windows, worlds apart when worlds

Like hearts can be so weak, collapsing at three in the mornimg
And going, for the the most part, unmourned. Picked over
By birds for bits of our past, tugging out tufts of hair
From the rubble, our bodies warm with worms like kisses.
Those are hers wriggling in me now, dancing in Havana.

MDP

PART 1
THE ORIGIN OF LIFE

The history of *McFadden Dairy Products*,
Beginning on the little farm out by the Corbett
And culminating in the construction in Las Vegas
Of the DNA Tower with its mile-high mast,

Is coterminous with the twenty-first century,
Revolving primarily around Margaret McFadden
And her partner 'in both business *and* pleasure',
Frank Y. McKinstry, with whom she was 'helically

Entwined' from the morning they met on the Gallbog Road,
When the ice got broke (it was Margaret broke it)
By the fact that they'd identical schoolbags, designed
To look like portable life supports, their NASA logos

Illuminated by so many red light-emitting diodes that even
A driver blind-drunk like the driver who killed Margaret's parents
Would have had no excuse for not seeing them when,
With their heads in the clouds of each other's incitements,

They sprinted together across the road, ducked through
A hole in the hedge and, leaving little footprints in the brittle,
White grass, as the bus roars by like a hothouse, vanished
Into the mist of a day which – having lasted for a quarter

Of a century – will find them, at its end, sitting cross-legged,
Eating blackberries in a field full of milkers, as the sun sets,
Jelly-red, like a Petri dish being held up to the sun
For inspection by the minds of two postgraduate students

In which the single greatest question burning there like death
Is beginning to break down under the action of bacteria and be
Redeployed, in front of their eyes, into the tiny green letters
At which they squint and exclaim, simultaneously, *Ulrika!*

PART 2

THE MOTORS

The kitchen is cold, despite the day having been so hot,
So Margaret gets down on her hands and her knees
And whistles to the ashes as her Daddy would have done
In the early hours of December 23rd, 2001

Had he not spent that night hand in hand with her Mum,
Singing for as long as he could, *What a friend we have in Jesus*,
In their little Morris Minor, its bonnet having bonded head-on with
The bonnet of a claret Mercedes, in the windscreen of which there's the face –

Like a sunset seen through melting frost – of the man so blinded by drink
He'd not even had the decency to close his eyes when, making full use
Of the width of the road, he'd met on a bend the lights of his death,
Dipped as they were, very kindly, in prayer … When her grip gives up

The ghost, turning colder than the coldness of the night, he spends
The last minutes of his life asking God to bless Margaret with His wisdom …
And so, as he would have done, she whistles, *This little light of mine*
Until flames like tongues in a meeting house arise and take up the refrain …

Frank does his bit with a bucket of coal and a copy of *Nature Genetics*
Which he's torn up and twisted like rope. When two mugs of tea later
They are sitting cross-legged, their laptops overheating on their laps,
The fire reflects on the polished flagstones until they float like two yogis

In a void, their eyeballs processing like barcodes as they whisper, *Holy cow!*
Or *Jasus!* … Or – and this coming only from Frank – *How's yer belly aff
Fer spats now, Ms McFadden?* To which Margaret replies by fixing him coolly,
One brow slightly raised and a withering, *I'm not sure I see your logic there, Jim.*

It is Margaret, being a good deal more worldly than Frank, who has thought
On ahead to the patent and the commercial exploitation of *Ulrika*, as the fire fades
Overwhelmed by the sun, slanting in from the wall of the scullery until it stands
Like a curtain between them or a mirror in which they each see their self as
    the other.

PART 3

THE HAND

Begun when she was 5 seconds old and completed 3 seconds later,
    ep-9.1's first great
Ground-breaking treatise was her ironically Marxist, 30-volume
    portrait of the bio-economic
Origins of *Ulrika*, entitled, *From the Corbett to the Back of Beyond*,
    culminating in a chapter
On Las Vegas and the planting of the DNA Tower which – being
    almost invisible in daylight,

Its mile-high mast appearing (at what is sometimes still thought of as
    sunset) to puncture
What remained of the breathable, like an arrow on its way to the
    future – she regarded as
A fitting memorial to the wet life of Margaret McFadden, whose
    boardroom battles with
Frank McKinstry were the subject of her second work, the poignant
    On a Farm in the Hills

Near Dromara, in which she charts the untwinning of their minds, up
    to and including his dramatic
Resignation on the eve of their landing on Mars, from which was to
    flow the first digital station
Based purely on the *Ulrika Protocol* with its tacit admission that the
    Earth was a goner,
Not a place where the future could be banked on to happen …
    Tch, banking! … thinks ep-9.1,

Smiling at the quaintness of the concept and the elegance with which
    McFadden had transcended it.
What a woman she was, she whispers, her lips only inches from the
    glass, as the tower revolves
From green to gold and, all around its mile-high mast, the *Turodecks*
    glitter, sticky like clouds
Of August midges … She turns away, tipping back what remains of
    her highball, and thinks

Hey, this ain't so bad, maybe I been missin out all these years ... She
    lights a cigarette – as Frank
Would have said – *for the higgle* and swaggers to the bedside mirror
    where head cocked, jut-jawed,
Looking down her nose and pretending to tote some Christ
    Almighty muthafucka of a weapon,
With the long strong Teutonic neck of the woman for whom there
    is no turning back, pectorals flexing

And the first faint sheen of sweat spreading on her breast like a
    breastplate, she winks, though not
At her own reflection but at the man whose hand I see before me
    now – darker perhaps than you
Would expect, with painted nails, a shaggy back and those
    extraordinary rings whose rocks
Refract the candlelight and unfurl rainbows round the walls which
    could as easily be cell walls

And not these walls of lacquered wood whose cracks let in not just
    the night but also this old
Lissom lizard who wades across the messy desk as if to read what
    you've been reading, has time
To shake its little head before being swept – *Too cruel!*– away by
    the hand whose final flourish stirs
So powerful a vortextual force the hand, the candle, desk, its mess
    get sucked down it, walls and all.

Light

C.K. WILLIAMS

Another drought morning after a too brief dawn downpour,
uncountable silvery glitterings on the leaves of the withering maples –

I think of a troop of the blissful blessed approaching Dante,
'a hundred spheres shining,' he rhapsodises, 'the purest pearls …'

then of the frightening brilliant myriad gleam in my lamp
of the eyes of the vast swarm of bats I found once in a cave,

a chamber whose walls seethed with a spaceless carpet of creatures,
their cacophonous, keen, insistent, incessant squeakings and squealings

churning the warm, rank, cloying air; of how one,
perfectly still among all the fitfully twitching others,

was looking straight at me, gazing solemnly, thoughtfully up
from beneath the intricate furl of its leathery wings

as though it couldn't believe I was there, or was trying to place me,
to situate me in the gnarl we'd evolved from, and now,

the trees still heartrendingly asparkle, Dante again,
this time the way he'll refer to a figure he meets as 'the life of …'

not the soul, or person, the *life*, and once more the bat, and I,
our lives in that moment together, our lives, our *lives*,

his with no vision of celestial splendour, no poem,
mine with no flight, no unblundering dash through the dark,

his without realising it would, so soon, no longer exist,
mine having to know for us both that everything ends,

world, after-world, even their memory, steamed away
like the film of uncertain vapour of the last of the luscious rain.

Adventures in Clubland

DON PATERSON

On Saturdays my father used to take me to Largs Music Supplies in the town to see the guitars he couldn't afford. The guitar department was in the basement, and was somewhere between a funeral parlour and a reptile house: two twilit, red-carpeted corridors arranged in a U, the guitars displayed in bright glass cases flush with the walls, where they reclined in proconsular luxury against waterfalls of peach and strawberry silks. They bore impossible prices, half a year's wages, and were as distant as another life. How badly I wanted these guitars for my father, those Gretsches, Gibsons, Guilds and Martins, those cathedrals of ebony and ash and maple and rosewood. We would walk down that underground street, stopping at every window to admire some bit of abalone purfling or intricate inlay, till we reached the counter at the turn of the U. There my father would talk lowly and sometimes darkly to Mr Dunn about his HP payment on whatever downmarket box he was playing that year. He did own the first Yamaha acoustic in Dundee, however – a surprisingly fine FG-180 which I eventually bought from him, then ruined through the grievously misguided practice of sanding down the soundboard until you could see the light through it. (This makes the instrument much louder, but weakens it fatally. Many who followed this briefly fashionable advice woke one morning to find the guitar had simply imploded under its 200-odd pounds of string tension. I saw an instrument do this once, sucked instantly into its own soundhole; it looked like *The Scream*.)

My father's loyalty over the years helped me land a part-time job

The Yellow Nib, Vol. 3, 2007, pp 51–68

there at fourteen. The place had changed to an ugly striplit stack-
'em-high emporium. The guitars were all out in the open now, as
they were no longer worth stealing. Mr Dunn was still at the helm, a
deeply straight but kindly old guy in pinstripes, from the era when
sales wasn't a consonantal rhyme for sleaze. Then there was Noel, the
coming man. Noel was a mustachioed Yorkshireman in a terrible
moiré suit woven from two shades of nylon, raspberry sauce and
algae, and resembled a giant bleeding frog. Noel was all twinkly
charm, and could've sold Gary Numan a ukulele, or Ian Paisley the
Dubliners Songbook. Anonymous among the Saturday staff was also
one Ged Grimes, later to re-emerge as the bassist with Danny
Wilson, who had a UK No. 1 with a divine pop song called Mary's
Prayer. Ged was the real thing, and therefore completely off the
radar. (Danny Wilson, named for the Sinatra film, were essentially
one guy called Gary Clark, a genius of a musician who sprang fully
formed from the empurpled thigh of the Fintry estate at seventeen.
Gary's only impediment to superstardom was that, while being
possessed of a voice like Marvin Gaye, the guitar chops of Jeff
'Skunk' Baxter and the songwriting skills of a Bacharach, he looked
like G.K. Chesterton in dungarees, and no amount of jaunty berets
and imaginative lighting could ever disguise this fact. I gather he
now spends his life in a windowless bunker in LA churning out hits
for nanotalents.)

Instead we were wowed by Steve, a nineteen-year-old, six-foot,
elfin-eared, feather-mulleted unisex dreamboat. Steve had been
drawn by Cocteau in an opium fug, with the other hand on his dick:
the roe-deer upper lip, the nose-job nose, the distracted myopia, that
particular kind of narcissistic melancholy that seems designed only to
convey that its wearer would, on the most inscrutable whim, fuck
anybody or anything – or indeed not fuck you for a million if you
were the last fuckable thing in the cosmos. His impossibly glamorous
weekends were torment to me. He was into 'experimental sex', and
loved to taunt me over my virginity, which I wore on my sleeve like
a black armband. I would labour over the careful arrangement of the
strings and capos and plectrums just to defer a little longer his usual
opener of 'So what did you get up last night.' Like that, without the
question mark. Me? Hell, I had arpeggiated the largely useless

maj7th#9#11 chord in seven positions and all keys, until I could see the fretboard pattern like a giant molecule as I fell asleep, and its intervals merged with whatever shape I was dreaming about folding Miss Walker (Latin) into. That's what I'd done, and I was keeping it to myself. 'Not much. And yourself, Steve,' I'd ask, although here the question mark was omitted more in sapped resignation than indifference to the reply. At least he made no pretence he was doing anything other than rubbing it in: Steve had done something in a jacuzzi in Carnoustie with identical twins and a dead puppy, or in a lift with two girls from Harris Academy and their PE teacher, or in his mum's bed with his aunt while his uncle beat off in the wardrobe, or – sick of the world and its need of him – on his own with a mirror and a noose and jar of meat.

— Still a virgin, Donald?

— Yup Steve. Still a virgin.

Immaculately coiffed and manicured, his skin bearing the light sheen and fragrance of some genderless posing grease, the cool oozed from Steve. He stole packets of strings and whole tubes of plectrums, flagrantly. He played in a post-punk band called Steve and the Somethings. (Punk went post- faster than anything. We couldn't wait to get it over.) Eventually, after much pleading from us, he played us a demo of a tune called 'We Got the Bottles in the Boot', being a lyric précis of some vodka-fuelled weekend sexual anabasis. It was an ugly thing, with Steve affecting the then obligatory Ian Dury accent. The Dundee accent is similar to Cockney in that there are few terminal consonants, and sentences are often just one long fluid vowel, interrupted by glottal stops. Thus a statement like *I ate all of it* – a common enough response amongst the Dundonian lower orders to most food-related enquiries – becomes *Eh ai' aa' o' i'*. Had Steve been from the estates, he would have managed it effortlessly. Had Steve been from the estates, he would also have been one of the stunted indigenous pizza-faced poor, though, i.e. not Steve. Being from good white-collar stock in Broughty Ferry, the chorus came out like *We gok the bokkles in the book*. Some horrible monosynth 'riff' buzzed away throughout, like a wasp stuck in a jamjar. Then Noel bravely pointed out most of the tune had been lifted straight from the Kinks' 'You Really Got Me'. Steve's white grease appeared to run a little, and proposed the ghost of a blush below; but he hardly missed a beat as his lovely upper lip curled like an exhausted wave, and he berated us for being so slow to rumble such a crude plagiarism. Somehow we were left feeling the stupid party again. Nonetheless I felt a strange creeping sensation I had not known before, and it therefore took me a while to name it: it was superiority.

Amongst the mass-produced East German clunkers and Taiwanese coffins that lined the walls were a couple of superb instruments, still unsold from ten years earlier. Looking at them translated me again to that old dark underworld Largs used to be, that gloomy lyre-emporium where folk would strike their Faustian deals, literally putting their health or marriage on the dotted line. Above all I coveted a lovely cherry-red Guild acoustic. It cost £450, a wholly fantastic sum. At quarter to five every Saturday, when the whole shop was still ringing from the last choked power chord from the last assault on 'Smoke on the Water', I'd plead with Mr Dunn for 'a wee go', and retire to the back room, bearing the Guild with preposterous care, like a Beefeater with a sceptre. There I'd do nothing more than play a few notes, and listen to them back. Good acoustic guitars, in my book, are all loud. Not for me those tinny, buzzy Nationals, or the Maccaferris that already sound like you're listening to them on a pre-war radio. There is an exquisite rule, though; the loudness is decreased as the action is decreased, the action being the space between the fretboard and the strings. An action of 1mm is as easy as air guitar, and in the hands of a decent musician feels like playing a kazoo; there's no resistance to the imagination. Alas, the thing is all but inaudible. At 2mm the character of the instrument starts to blossom, but the strings also offer a fair old resistance; 3mm, and the guitar fully signs its own acoustic signature, it becomes its own church, its own auditorium, a self-amplifying miracle. By then, though, it's a perfect agony to play. The hardcore – mainly US redneck bluegrass flatpickers with huge Martin dreadnoughts – string their guitars like pianos, keep squash balls in their left pockets, coat their fingertips in superglue, and bugger each other angrily in the woods. The cherry-red Guild, though, was set up on the middle-way principle, an angel of a guitar fallen gracefully amongst the world of men. A run of notes sounded as clear as water, and every chord was so much fairy campanology. Steve heard me practise and screwed up his pretty nose. 'It's all just *runs*, isn't it.' It was indeed all just runs, but I knew what they had cost me, and so did he.

One Saturday, Steve didn't ask his usual question, for which I was grateful; but then I grew curious at his silence, so I asked him. He was vulnerably greaseless that day and clearly fighting back the tears, so I didn't push it. I learned later from Noel – in whom he'd foolishly confided – that Steve, during one of his Friday night pile-ons, had been enthusiastically bummed by an uninvited third or possibly fifth party but thought it uncool to protest. There are noble reasons why a woman or a man might allow themselves to suffer such a thing, but the Preservation of Cool isn't one of them. Even Steve seemed to register this, and thereafter he was a little broken, which is to say he behaved a little better.

Alas, I was starting to behave a little worse. To say I had no social skills would be too generous. I had negative capability, and every conversational gambit was the mere conjecture of a shipwrecked Venusian. I had heard somewhere that slagging folk off was good because men liked to unite round a common grievance, and that swearing was good too, but hadn't heard the bit that said the Alphas have to choose the target and set the tone. I would regale the male staff and most of the customers with much comradely f-ing and c-ing, and was soon taken aside by the worldly Noel, who was kind enough to sketch in the first few rules of human society. By then, though, I'd left myself with too much ground to make up.

And although I could shift a mean plectrum, the bigger sales were passing me by. Guitars were sold the way Noel sold them, by brute force, or the way Steve sold them, by playing the first four bars of the dreadful 'Theme from *The Deer Hunter* Otherwise Known as Cavatina or He Was Beautiful', then shooting a conspiratorial look at the buyer – raised eyebrow, lopsided half-smile, a kind of inaudible microsnort – whereupon they both tacitly agreed the fifth bar was below him, and does this guitar work or *what*. I knew, though, the fifth bar was also beyond him, and he knew I knew. Mr Dunn also knew I knew, but requested, reasonably, that I also learn the first four bars of 'Cavatina', from *Steve*. Demonstrating shite Chinese three-quid guitars by a violent burst of one of my favourite intervallic studies (I had still not actually learned a *tune*) was not likely to impress a mother who only wanted it so her wee girl could learn the chords in the Grease Songbook. As I would have eaten Steve's tapeworm before I'd have taken a guitar lesson from him, I flatly refused, and sealed my fate. Mr Dunn soon informed me that Central Office had directed him to lose staff, and as I had been there the shortest time it was with great regret, and all that. I believed him, and so suffered no great loss of pride. Foolishly returning the following Saturday for a chat with the guys, I was at the foot of the stairs when I caught the sugary-sick strains of 'Cavatina' again, and quickly registered that the performer was at least ten bars into it. I turned round and went home, trying to remember if they'd used it at that bit where Christopher Walken shoots himself in Saigon. Because they fucking should have.

Three years later. An early brush with a particularly demented brand of charismatic Christianity, followed by a psychotic episode triggered by a three-day out-of-body experience after some very bad hash landed me in hospital for four months. The trouble with depression is that the climb back is much harder than the descent: the descent is a breeze. It is also one of those few occasions where the directional metaphor is perfectly accurate, culturally unrevisable: in despair, gravity intensifies. The dreams are all of falling. Given the agonising 24-point plans I was pursuing to get the better of my now rampant agoraphobia, how on earth I decided that the stage was the only place it could be kept in check is a mystery. I had worked as my father's rhythm accompanist since I was fifteen or so, though, and I guess he must have dragged me along one evening to help set up the PA, just to get me out the house. I found, standing on that raised semicircle again, that the psychic palisade I had spent years laboriously nailing together was still intact: I am, like my father, temperamentally unqualified for this kind of work, and the strong defensive reflexes we develop to compensate are a long time in fading. So I felt at my safest where you might feel at your least, i.e. at the St Mary's Country and Western Club on a Tuesday night, standing under the Confederate flag playing Elvis's 'Trilogy' (or 'Triology', to give its local pronunciation): 'Dixie' / 'Hush Little Baby Don't You Cry' / 'Mine Eyes Have Seen the Glory', while a solemn ring of cowboys and gals stood below me, their eyes closed and their Stetsons doffed and their hands on their hearts, firing off their replica Smith & Wessons as it reached its gloopy climax.

On these nights I was technically invalidating my invalidity benefit, but I needed my therapy, my weekly dose at the isotope of tiny fame; it would have taken far too long to explain to the angry DHSS doctor who grudgingly (too light a word: it positively grieved him to do so) renewed my claim every few months. Eventually, about a year later and apoplectic with what he correctly saw as my malingering, he sent me for 'retraining' at the rehabilitation centre. This involved a week of 'assessment', which consisted of laying a path of paving slabs that went absolutely nowhere. The slabs themselves were removed from another path to a different nowhere built the week before. If you collapsed, or demonstrated a genuinely terminal incompetence, you'd be sent to receive some training in light clerical work. After one morning in this gloomy Tartarus spent imagining the afternoon, I reclassified myself as unemployed, and set about honestly not looking for work.

Signing on was no humiliation, unless you'd been working the C&W clubs the night before and were recognised by the clerk. However, the chances of them challenging your claim were pretty remote, since it would have entailed a more embarrassing disclosure on their part – i.e. that they had spent Tuesday night kitted out as Wyatt Earp or Calamity Jane. Once or twice we exchanged a resigned shrug, but that was as much grief as I received. Anyway my father – inspired by one phaser-drenched machine-gun solo on an Indian raga in 'Truck Drivin' Man' that lost him his next booking at Lochee Gunslingers – soon forced me to answer a small ad in the *Dundee Courier*. The Management were looking for a new lead guitarist.

I went along to the Fairmuir Social Club to meet the band and the outgoing guitarist, Jock: a genial, rough-as-fuck, good-looking mustachioed outlaw-type. He played well enough in the Gregg Allman style everyone in Dundee was strangely obsessed with at the time, and was leaving the band, he told me without irony, to concentrate more seriously on his drinking. I did the machine-gun raga solo on 'Once, Twice, Three Times a Lady'. Jock – a muso, and thus capable of terrible suspensions of taste – was impressed, and his word carried some authority, despite the rest of the band's reasonable misgivings. I was in. Jock stayed on for a couple of weeks to show me the ropes.

Jock was also the first person I had ever seen who was *brilliant* with women. His spectacular success, I observed – hell, I was taking notes and abstracting formulae – was down to one thing I realised the others conspicuously lacked: he really *liked* them. By any normal yardstick, the success of the rest of the Management was also spectacular, but anyone in a clubbie band who couldn't get laid three times a week was either a clinical sociopath (like me; technically I really *was*) or had some weeping facial elephantiasis (like Shug McCafferty of our near-rivals Jack Black and the Sweetie Tray, who performed in shadow, by popular request). In those days nearly all male musicians regarded it less as a perk than a responsibility: to not shag *all* the time was an abuse of privilege equivalent in its perversity to a council bus driver paying his fare home, and was deeply frowned upon as a betrayal of the whole guild. The strange cachet conferred merely by randomly hitting an instrument while standing one foot higher than the rest of the audience, dressed in what would be wholly inappropriate for one foot lower, says a lot both about the social function of glamour and its highly relative nature. Sometimes just *owning* an instrument was enough. One celebrated case involved an alto player from Kirkton, a man of legendary concupiscence, who had worked for years in the horn section of a local R&B covers band. One day he had joined his colleagues in the studio to record a demo. Despite his pleas that it would 'ruin the collective vibe', the horns were all mic'ed up individually. However after an hour the engineer – after much beard-scratching and checking of cables – could get nothing but spill and silence from the alto mic; finally the altoist broke down and admitted that he had not played a single note in his entire career, nor could, and left weeping hot tears of shame. Rather touchingly, he was rehired almost immediately; the band all felt his leaving had subtracted a certain sexual *je-ne-ken-what* from the live act. He was back on the stand, bequiffed and huffing air, by the following weekend.

Jock's braggadocio was as gross as the rest of the band's – but while their chat-ups were conducted as public performances, whenever Jock talked to a woman everyone else in the room disappeared. I once watched him score from literally thirty yards. All he did was catch the eyes of a girl at the bar; the two of them then proceeded to stare each other out, the way those wonderful people do. She lost her nerve first, though, disguising it as a behind-hand aside to her neighbour. 'Ye bastard – Won!' Jock yelled, and punched the air. She laughed. He laughed. The band laughed too, but he was laughing with her, not us. After the gig she was carrying his guitar case out to the car while he wound up his leads.

I think the band knew deep down I was the wrong guy for the job, though, and my ant-infested solos were totally inappropriate for the simpler terrain of 'Stand and Deliver' and 'Karma Chameleon'. Nonetheless the speed I could deliver the notes at was enough to blind weaker musicians to the order, and I had the sense to keep it from getting too outré. But I considered the popular music of the era beneath contempt, and I would approach the guitar solo from 'Hotel California' less with cynicism than a sense of doing my bit for interplanetary relations. Christ knows, it must have sounded like it. However, at least my sound had improved: Jock sold me his Fender Twin Reverb outrageously cheaply – pitying me, correctly, for my awful tranny H&H amp-head and the speaker cabs my Dad had made from chipboard. The Fender Twin, in those days, was a giant box full of Russian valves and weighed like the Ark of the Covenant. Compared with the H&H, it also *felt* like plugging in to the Ark of the Covenant, and was the difference, acoustically, between opening your lungs in St Martin-in-the-Fields or a chip shop. And – much like the Ark of the Covenant, I'd imagine – it also had the great advantage of staying hot for two hours after the gig. Several times I found myself outside the closing club, perched on the amp for warmth, and clearing a perfect black circle from the snow while I waited for the cab. (Years later, I watched a programme where an eighty-year-old Kung Fu master stood in a field of snow and melted everything within a six-foot radius, and it took me a moment to locate the familiarity of the scene.) The alternative to the cab was the lift home, which could take hours, as I was inevitably left in the car to mind the gear while the keyboard player or whoever dropped off some lonely rig-widow with glitter on her décolletage for a nightcap and a leisurely hump on the sofa.

Much of the time was spent in transit, in the back of the Transit. What a piece of real onomastic genius: the Transit was a terrible cipher, a 70mph brain-juddering purgatory which ceased to exist when it stopped moving; no one in their right mind would spend a second longer inside than they had to. In Transit, the culture was established firmly on the hierarchy of male needs: food/sex/games pretty much covers it. The standard of the conversation was never high, but In Transit it soon turned Molloy-like in its hollow repetitions. The usual destination of the Transit was a wedding out of town. Shag-wise they were highly specialised affairs, and had a scoring system – 2 for a ride, 4 for a bridesmaid, 6 for the bride's mum, 8 for the maid of honour. In my time, there was only one verified claim on the perfect 10. The gig was, inevitably, in Fife: Fife, last bastion of the Picts, whose broad face and beaky nose I bear. The social immobility of certain parts of its population has resulted in a level of feral inbreeding too dangerous for scientific survey: there are settlements in Central Fife which make the Pitcairn Islands look like the West Village. Hoards of identically ugly children – who by rights should all be *singularly* ugly – will eat the legs of any traveller stupid enough to pause to ask directions. Weddings, and hence the presence of visiting sperm from Tayside, therefore represented unmissable opportunities to enhance the gene pool. It was the drummer's call: in the van, in the car park, between the meal and the evening dance. The bride called it, with questionable timekeeping, her 'last wee fling'. He kept the garter and wore it on his head as a sweatband, after the happy couple had been waved off into the night.

The Management also gave me my first studio experience: we went in to record Jeff's self-penned number, 'Motel'. The rest of the band were into soul and funk, but our lead singer and bandleader was the only guy who really shared the tastes of our audience, and was a huge Rod Stewart fan. 'Motel' was a shamelessly derivative fag-hoarse she-done-me-wrong anthem. After the third chorus of

'Mo-tel, sheez treatin' me laark a mo-tel (*in-an-outta-gen*)' I had one eight-bar guitar break, and I filled it with many notes. The guy on the desk was impressed, if no one else was. The studio was plastered with the promo flyers of previous clients. Jim Jackannelli was an accordionist forever getting accidentally booked as a trio, and then sent home by disappointed promoters. The Threepenny Tray were a kind of poor man's Barron Knights, or would have been, had their impersonations borne the slightest relation to the impersonated; you could watch an entire set and remain wholly oblivious to that dimension of their performance. Bonny and Ronny were the pond life of the club scene. Bonny was very far from, an afro'd boss-eyed plane-crash of a lass in specs like two fishbowls, while Ronny was an essay in hair, dandruff, paisley pattern, green corduroy and soup stains. They specialised in songs in praise of specific council estates – 'Fintry's the Schemie for Me'; 'My Heart is in West Kirkton'; 'Mid Craigie's the Schemie for Me'; and 'When I Get Back to Fintry' (presumably from Mid Craigie) – in limited-edition Christmas releases sold in hand-made cardboard dump-bins in strategic outlets, as well as covers of songs they didn't know, with a have-a-go attitude wholly commendable in its lunatic bravery. My friend 'Big' Rab Adams swears he heard someone request the Hank Williams classic 'Your Cheatin' Heart' at a wedding Bonny and Ronny had been hired to compère. 'Your cheatin' heart,' Ronny gamely essayed, 'Your cheatin' heart … your cheatin' heart; your cheatin' heart…', the rest of the song drowned in abuse and exploding pint glasses. The first time they had been in to the studio, Ronny had asked for his finished demo. For a laugh, the engineer scraped up a handful of bits of old quarter-inch tape from the floor, and handed them to Ronny. Ronny, a child of God, in his way, thanked him, cheerfully stuffed the knotted mess in his pocket and walked straight out into the street.

The WOL, or Wee Orange Light, was a particularly dreaded feature of certain clubs, and many bands refused to play in rooms fitted with them. The wee orange light was a device that the council could forcibly install if enough noise-related complaints were gathered from local residents. It would flicker three times if a certain decibel threshold was reached, and on the third a power-breaker would be triggered and cut the supply to the stage. This would not only risk

surges that would blow the valves on your lovingly reconditioned
Vox AC30, but destroy all the presets in your DX7 that had taken you
three months to program. It was usually accompanied by several
bangs, flashes and clouds of coloured smoke from exploding
equipment, and was invariably mistaken for an unusually tight
ending complete with stage pyrotechnics, thus sending the crowd
into delirious ovation. Indeed, if it occurred towards the end of the
evening that's just how you would pass it off, ignoring the cries for an
encore while you hunted for the fire extinguishers. Three numbers
in, though, the effect was less desirable. The entire band would end
up watching the wee orange light throughout the gig, waiting for the
second flicker that would place us on our final warning; thereafter we
would turn down to an inaudible tinkle, and the drummer would
switch to brushes for 'Eye of the Tiger', which was then sung like a
barbershop quartet hired to serenade your dying mother. Five pairs of
eyes locked on the wee bulb, arguments of the *aye-it-did-no'-it-didnae*
type would break out continually – and if it *did* flicker, who had been
responsible. In our case it was usually Glen, the bass player, a nice but
deeply insecure and bumptious lad with a weight and aftershave
problem, and an accidental Hitler moustache. Glen was given to
terribly mistimed boutades of overenthusiasm, particularly in his
backing vocals, where things would come out much sooner and ten
times louder than he'd intended. Thus, in 'The Theme from Fame':
   — Erv-uh-ree dayyyeee is lak sur …
   — SURVAAHVAL!!
   — Fuck's sake.
   — Sorry lads.
Later:
   — *Arm gonna leerve for eh-eh-vurr, am gonna lurn howdda fl…*
   — *FAME!!*
   — Fuck's sake.
   — Sorry lads.
   — *And* ye've set that fuckin light aff again ye fat prick.
   — Huvnae.
   — Huv.
   — Huv *nutt*.
   — Huv *sutt*.

— Huv *nutt!*

— Huv *SUTT!*

KAABANG!! (followed by mass cheering)

— Aw for fuck's sake.

— Davie!

— What?

— Yer wah wah pedal's on fire.

The Management might have been a little under-rehearsed at times, but compared to the geriatric Bob Skelly Combo we were drilled like the SAS. Having first ok'd it with Jeff, who viewed all other bands as the enemy, I accepted a few gigs while their 100-a-day guitarist recovered from the subtraction of his remaining leg. Bob was an accordionist turned Cordovox player. They asked if I could read, which was a promising sign; I said yeah, a bit, if I got the charts before the gig. They arrived in the post. By 'read', Bob had meant 'the alphabet'. The 'charts' were bits of paper ripped from a school jotter, each tune consisting of a row of large letters to indicate the order in which the chords should occur – but, in the absence of bar lines, no indication as to when. (The 'when', I later discovered on the gig, I was to take from the bassist's cues, which he gave in a series of violently mimed headbutts. The fast ska chord changes of Madness's 'Baggy Trousers' induced a near-blackout, though, and he had to complete the song sitting down.)

Their regular gig was the old Dundee FC Supporters Club. I arrived an hour early, as agreed, for a run-through of the material. I couldn't get in as there was a fight in the foyer; two drunks had pulled knives on each other and were frozen in stand-off. Someone called upstairs, and a five-foot MC in a Zapata 'tache, frilly shirt and plum velvet suit with matching bowtie came down to sort things out. He said nothing, but merely opened the left side of his jacket: in the inside pocket was a small axe. The two men muttered their apologies and shook hands. Then they let them both *in*.

I headed for the dressing room and got changed into the band uniform, or as near as I could get it – my old way-too-tight school trousers and a black nylon shirt of my Dad's. The band had conceived the idea, which I have encountered several times since, that black shirts are a charm against BO, on the principle they don't seem to need much washing. Five minutes after we were due to go on, the rest of the band showed up. Although initially annoyed, I soon saw the pointlessness of the run-through. The Bob Skelly Combo were an education in what could pass for music amongst the tone deaf. I once had a conversation with Mícheál Ó Súilleabháin on this subject: his theory was that as long as there was something resembling a tune and a regular rhythm, you could harmonise a song like Boulez or Cecil Taylor, and a rustic audience would have no strong objections – being less indifferent to harmony than wholly oblivious to its existence. (Towards the end of the evening the tune itself could be abandoned, and a random series of notes substituted; as long as you could still dance to it, all would be well.) This indeed was pretty much Bob's approach. Bob, like Cecil Taylor, had also driven a cab to subsidise his art; but the harmonic freedoms Cecil had won through years of intense study and cautious experiment, Bob had achieved instantly, through the simple expedient of not giving a fuck. His left hand was like the upper body of Irish dancers, present but terminally infarcted; it was simply dragged along for the ride. It crashed and bumped around on the bottom half of his keyboard like an ancient trailer on a loose tow-bar, and aspired to no greater accuracy or accomplishment in life than scratching his balls.

The drummer was also something of an innovator, and had a specially constructed kit, with a ring-holder for his pint and an ashtray welded to the tom stand; in place of the second tom, he had welded the top half of a music stand, on which he'd place a copy of *Hustler* or an Edge Western. The difficult procedure of turning the pages while playing was brilliantly solved by stopping playing, and then turning the page. I could always tell when he was on prose, as the drop-outs grew farther apart. He had three fingers on either hand – the result, he told me, of a sawmill accident. (I swear to God this is true, having heard it subsequently repeated as an urban myth.) The first finger was lost when a plank slipped under a bandsaw. The second finger was lost demonstrating how he'd cut off the first.

I have heard covers bands in South East Asia who produce immaculate live versions of songs the original artists had taken months in the studio to perfect, and would themselves be incapable of delivering. Bob was the exact antithesis, and given to the most spectacular approximation. There was nonetheless a kind of genius of economy here: knowing the two or three bits of the tune by which his cloth-eared audience might – by whatever somnambulant verification procedure – identify it, he would present these as semi-random prompts, while the rest of the song fell into an atonal mishmash. The most important bit was the intro, when everyone feels the sugar-rush of recognition, security and reassurance; this was often accompanied by cheers of relief. Then there was the middle bit; so as long as 'Karma Chameleon' went *karmakarmakarmakarmakarma kamee-lee-yon* at some point, you were home and dry. But if you really wanted to ingratiate yourself, you would end abruptly together, anywhere and on any note. This was taken as a sign of a thorough professionalism the audience would dimly pride themselves on being able to recognise, and the jolt administered would provoke spontaneous and wild applause. In this anti-aesthetic there was only one possible criticism: *for fuck's sake play somethin' wih ken*; and one possible compliment: *yous lads werenae too loud nor nothin*. Between the whirlpool and rock of bewilderment and irritation, the Bob Skelly Combo steered an unerring and masterly course.

They were also responsible for some of the most bestial sex I have ever witnessed on a gig. I once stumbled in on the drummer and a lass getting it together on a radiator in the dressing room. She was, considerately, holding the drummer's pint.

— Sorry son, we'll no' be a minute.

— Aye Wullie – I'd better get back. I telt ma Mum I was just awa for a pish.

— Hang on lass – nearly there – gnaaaaaagh!

— Fuck for that.

— See ye efter?

— Maybe ye will, maybe ye winna.

— Oh ye wee *tease*.

Another involved three band members and one very accommodating granny. Technically speaking I suppose they were enacting in live tableaux one of those later chapters in the *Perfumed Garden*, where the woman demonstrates the simultaneous pleasuring of many men, though it looked more like a game of Twister gone terribly wrong at a hospice Christmas party. Usually such liaisons involve three contortionists and one uncomfortable woman, but the woman looked like the only comfortable one here, decorsetted and relaxed in her open gussets, while three scarlet-faced arthritic wrecks wheezed away in their shirt tails and socks. Davie raised his hand in a pained gesture of greeting, and possibly invitation, but aside from the orifice-shortage (it would have involved doubling up somewhere) and as desperate as I was to lose my virginity, this was so far off the scale of acceptable ticks I passed immediately.

I only ever visited one club in Dundee lower down the food chain. It was a surreal evening anyway. I had, improbably, turned up at the wrong gig on the wrong night with what turned out to be an empty guitar case – like some Zen fable, the point of which was lost on me. I saw a neighbour I knew, and he bought me a half. The place was a long, low-ceilinged windowless bunker between the two worst schemes in the city. The dim orange uplighters gave it the look of a torch-lit crypt, and concealed its filthy plush and scorched carpet. It was obviously a condition of membership that you had to be able to walk upright under a parked artic and emerge with your bonnet still straight: at 5'8" I was a titan. Everyone was either silent or comatose with drink, though some would rouse themselves to a brief incoherent rage every ten minutes or so. The club was strictly Men Only – a superfluous edict if ever there was one; though this was in place not because of their chauvinism, which would have required the energy to sustain a prejudice in the first place, but because sex or its distraction wasn't even a *thought* for them. Sex is at least a sign of being alive, in some recognisable way. A student of tantra might have said that their kundalini had now retracted to lie coiled at the base of the spine, at the muladhara chakra, where man becomes a kind of mobile plant-life. They all died there, in the club, on the floor or in the toilet or slumped at the table, and their friends took three hours to notice.

At the age of nineteen I was also working with a wee band I kept secret from Jeff called Ghosts, named for an Albert Ayler tune which sounds like a cross between a Sousa march and a demonic invocation. We were a trio, and we had about four and a half numbers I'd written, which I could barely play. Among them, I recall, were 'Elephant Rut', 'Titular Absence' and 'My Italics'. Our drummer, Doug, had, as they say, a lot of shit worked out in 7/8, but actually much less in 4/4. He would play 4/4 in multiples of 28, and every seven bars we would coincide, like those trains on the underground you suddenly find yourself riding parallel with for a few cheery seconds, before plunging back into the lonely dark. We had a wee poster drawn by an Art School pal of my girlfriend's, strange scribbly figures drawn from the inside out. We played a couple of gigs under UV lighting in wee back rooms in the Dundee stoner quarter, to much nodding of heads.

When Jeff found out about the existence of Ghosts he went berserk at my perfidy, and threatened to sack me. I sat him down and put on a tape of our last gig. His face was at first horrified, then it contorted in pity. He raised his palm to signal he'd had enough (it was halfway through the free-improv arco bass solo in 'Titular Absence', and frankly so had I) and then spoke to his inturned fingernails.

— Don.

— Aye?

— Look man. I ken ye've had a hard time. Like ...

— What?

— Like when ye were in the hospital and aa that.

— Oh aye.

— We'll no' say anything to the other lads aboot this.

— Cheers man.

Ghosts was never mentioned again. However, now my dark jazz secret was out in the open, the fun was gone. Even if no one else gave a hoot over my lack of note-for-note sincerity, I found, implausibly, that I did. The Management had started to kill my playing, and I quit practising. Ghosts evaporated in a cloud of bong-smoke; I think Doug discovered 4/4 and joined another clubbie band. The bassist changed his name, implausibly, to Nico and joined the Proclaimers. The end came with astonishing swiftness one night in the St Joseph's Club. I was, from the vantage of the high stage, watching a lad in a dark corner manually bringing his girl to a climax while he read the back of the *Courier*; a particularly ugly fight had broken out over the pool table, and a guy was being forced to admit the black ball into his mouth. We were halfway through Barry Manilow's 'Bermuda

Triangle'. I could hear Jeff singing somewhere far below me, as from
the bottom of a well. *Burmoo-da trah-yangle | It makes people dizz -peer
… Burmoo-da trah-yangle …* One bar into my guitar solo, I suffered
what can only be described as an acute failure of the will, and found
myself unable to play a note. It was identical to a panic attack, with
the usual choking sensation and bird's-eye view of myself, except I
didn't actually *care*. It was a relief to be out of it – my body, this club,
this life, this particular fuckawful song. Jeff turned his head slowly
towards me to meet my lifeless stare, and all was instantly
understood. I fired myself on the spot.

> Bermuda Triangle
> It makes people disappear
> Bermuda Triangle
> Don't go too near
> But look at it from my angle
> And you'll see why I'm so glad
> Now Bermuda Triangle
> Not so bad
>
> B. MANILOW

In the Adriatic

CHRIS AGEE

NIGHT FERRY

Sad panda features, the old man atilt in the Full Moon:
Where is the lunar phosphorescence of the first crossing?

AUGUST GHOST

At the table on the veranda, or my laptop upstairs,
The neighbour's Amazonian green parrot haunts me

With sudden child's-cries of *Jacob! ... Jacob! ... Jacob!*
Mimicking, I swear, the very voice of Miriam

Trailing her brother in the garden four summers before.

KEEPSAKES

White Dalmatian sailor's cap (child-splattered), pen shell,
Partisan bullet, playing cards, Miriam's blue plastic teapot,

A piece of sea-worn copper shaped like a verdigris cedilla
Or the Mediterranean's inverted questionmark: the sacred

Objects of dead summers in the stone house at Zrnovo.

The Yellow Nib, Vol. 3, 2007, pp 69–72
© Chris Agee

ZEPHYR

Nightmountain against the sky's lighter leaven. The Mistral
Blows through the waiting village, speaking of rainstorms

And old sorrow, bringing coolth to the limestone casement.

NEAR DUBROVNIK

Ragusa chalked in black on the back of the chest-of-drawers
Shifted from its corner. Mid-August beer with Slobodan:

Did it first come to the house, we wonder, from Italy
During the bleak afterlife of Occupation and Resistance?

SEA CLOUD

Golden-lettered, on the bowsprit of a wooden schooner,
Inevitable coinage I had never heard, or imagined:

Your memory as beautiful and distant, horizon-floating
On the blues of a thousand days launched without you.

DARWINIAN SCRABBLE

Looking down, I find the Adriatic cross-spider's back's
A crusader's tunic reminding me of the photograph

I saw once in a natural history of endangered Hawai'i
Of the *Hawaiian Happy-Face Spider* whose own amazing

Back might be whole days of life together I can't remember.

TALISMAN

This summer, a small praying mantis found its way
To the linens of Jacob's bed. It was wan and dying

But held on for three days in our makeshift glass nautilus
Before expiring clutching a bed of fennel and dead ants.

NIGHTSKY

Are they really all up there, in the Evangelical distance? True
To the thing I do – metaphor's dark matter – I see in the
    Milky Way

A badger's stripe, one ring of Saturn, its cue-ball of astrophysics.

IN THE HAMMOCK

Like death the *Tremontana* came over the mountains
Out of Bosnia, empurpling the dark Balkan storm

As it did the halfmoons of your fingernails. Next day
Was rinsed-out, swept-clean clarity. Against the azure

A fractal branching of leaves in the breezy walnut
Trembled with dapple. But Angelo's almond, and the old

Hackberry at the grotto, were lost to the world forever.

LOVE

You will never return. Hope means nothing
And nothing will alter it. Love means something

Though: *you still exist for me*. Like the Big Dipper
Between the void of the two cypress, or a day moon

Against the shimmering stavelines of the heart's pylon.

THE BENCH

We are leaving you again. The way we did
The day of the crematorium, or on the plane

To London. Your bench must weather
Another year of summer sun, winter rains,

Long nights in the maquis solitudes above
The twinking necklace of the Old Town. I feel

You're there always in the offing, waiting
An eternity for our evening walks. How lonely

The dead are, keeping time's vigil for our return.

SEA SNAIL

I was thinking of enchantments: Odysseus at Defora
Shouldering his ship to a strange shore, thirsty still

For life, keen for sweet water and wild boar,
Projecting the gods and forces onto the island

Of scrub-oak and Aleppo over the glistening bay.
A moment later, we find a delicate Adriatic shell,

Our most beautiful ever, back blanched and bossed,
The inner whorl the colour of a cameo's porphyry.

Three Poems

LEONTIA FLYNN

Elizabeth Bishop

Darkness is falling on Worcester, Massachusetts.
Shadows lengthen. The sun slinks past the rooftop
and drops out of sight. Elizabeth has bronchitis.
And asthma. And eczema.
                              'Kidnapped'
from safety, the door which she heard slam
(her mother won't return from the institution)
slams for her too. She thinks it says her name:
orphan, depressive, drinker, lesbian –

and soon-to-be veteran loser. Losing
is many attractive locations – Maine
New York, and (scene of her near-death
brush with a cashew) Brazil …
lost parents, houses: she'll lose exceptionally well,
lover by lover. She even loses her breath.

Robert Lowell

1

The milky light of a lobster town in Maine
Is light thrown by water. Bleak light. Robert Lowell
in middle age is frizzled stale and sane.
He feels his ill-spirit sob in each blood cell.

Back in his childhood were parental rows
really responsible for this big rebellion
against the line – that twists and tangles now –
of Protestantism, of literary tradition,

against the tide of caste marine-blue blood
and *politics*? This government-made warfare
could, in its turn, hardly seem less mad
than mania's 'magical orange grove in a nightmare':
the murdered boys and their returning shrouds
spurring his hell-raising-poet's un-scared stare.

2

But imagine leaving his third and unreal wife
in order to return to his suffering second:
revising and revising
as though they were just lines or matters of form

the living details of a living life?
And imagine using those letters in his sonnets?
Using and reusing
the fact of pain – as though pain were a poem;

or as though (old story)
life and art
were, for this poet, as minutely clocked

as his dramatic final taxi journey
(as his heart
in his body) when both stopped.

Saturday in the Pool

The boy pauses at the end of the diving board
then dives: a broad sword
cleaving the water – there is parting! And rejoining!
This is reflected back upon the ceiling
where, flippered, supine
– swimming in the cells
and water-pathways of ourselves –
we watch the gases breed: a fog of chlorine.

The boy pauses at the end of the diving board
Then dives: on board
The Liberator, big-eyed airmen watch
as the cargo leaves the hatch:
the missile stabs the air
then impacts – megavolts
and gigawatts, primordial lightning bolts –
in whirlpool ripples: clouds of dust and vapour.

Saturday at the pool. A dozen forms
Push. Kick. Breathe. Push. Kick. Breathe. Turn
and bring themselves along the tepid length
and breadth of the translucent element
like frogmen. Bone
and blood. Four dozen limbs
– nurses, teachers, wives – civilians.
Push. Kick. Breathe. Push. Kick. Breathe. Turn

Outside our youth is laid about the park.
Planes thread the sky like needles. No attack
presents itself. No dogfight
twists on above the level of the trees. A kite
is moored in the sky. It peers,
like the boy on the diving board, down upon the world
where we have crawled: we are raw-gilled
and live. The blood is banging in my ears.

('Live' in the last line is the adjective, rhyming with 'five'.)

Not Being There[*]
(Or Nil–Two Desperandum)

GLENN PATTERSON

There is a school of thought in football (and if the words 'school', 'thought' and 'football' made you smirk you might be interested to know there are poems and stories on other pages), a school of thought in football that says the only real fan is the fan who goes week after week to watch his team in the flesh: the wet Wednesday night Carling Cup away match as well as the home European glamour tie. By this definition I cannot claim to be a real fan. I have supported Manchester United since I was five years old, yet at the age of forty-five I have seen them play only six times, one of them a pre-season friendly in which so many youth team players were fielded I could have been watching a mass *Jim'll Fix It* for eleven wee lads from down our park.

For maybe twenty of those forty years the only football matches guaranteed to be carried live on television were the FA Cup Final and the annual England v Scotland home international. Of course there were the weekly highlights programmes – *Match of the Day* on BBC, and ITV's *Big Match* – but in those days before Sky removed the limits (and simultaneously narrowed the focus on to the 'big four' clubs) it was rare for any team to feature more than one week in every five or

---

*   With a nod to Jerzy Kosinski, who takes it on his thigh, swivels ... In your dreams, Kosinski, in your dreams.

The Yellow Nib, Vol. 3, 2007, pp 76–82
© Glenn Patterson

six. Ulster Television took its *Big Match* from London Weekend Television, so Belfast fans could only hope to see United when they came to The Capital and even then it was just as likely you would switch on to find Gillingham entertaining Shrewsbury at the Priestfield Stadium in the old fourth division.*

But, then, my father supported Hibernians and Arsenal as a boy and never saw either of them, could hardly imagine the circumstances in which he would get to see them. A match was a composite experience, assembled over two, even three days, starting with the reports in *Ireland's Saturday Night*, aka the *Ulster*. At least when I was growing up we had Radio 2 clearing its Saturday afternoon schedules to bring updates from around The Country, which we listened to while attending matches in our own not-quite-country or even turning out in games ourselves. (Our goalkeeper's second-most important task was making sure the transistor behind his goalpost didn't get hit by the ball.) And then there was the legendary Teleprinter, stuttering across the *Grandstand* screen every Saturday from twenty to five, leaving a week's worth of hopes dashed or intact in its wake:

> 4.44 Man United 1 Southampton stutter-stutter-stutter ohplease-ohplease-ohplease (because the Teleprinter was the first machine I thought was responsive to prayer, or at least to side-deals with God) oh-please-let-it-be-nil-and-I-will-never-again-use-bad-language stutter-stutter-stutter 0
> Thank fuck, Frank Bough!

It was a rare event to arrive at half past ten on a Saturday night and *Match of the Day* without some knowledge of the afternoon's goings-on. We earned pocket money delivering *Ulster*s (because some institutions are sacrosanct), and even if you tried not to turn to the back page where the English scores were to be found there was always the possibility that a fan of a rival team would give you a broad intimation of how things had gone: 'Jammy bastards the day!' or, more succinctly, 'Up your hole!'

Midweek matches were a different matter. Midweek matches were

---

* More likely, if anything: the *Big Match*'s main commentator, Brian Moore, was a Gillingham director.

the source of the newsreader's injunction to 'look away now' if you wanted to avoid seeing the score before the highlights came on. Often, though, it was possible to predict the arc, if not the precise outcome, of a game from just a brief look at the highlights themselves. So Manchester United take on Wolverhampton Wanderers at Molyneux in the replayed quarter-final of the FA Cup, March 1976. The highlights start at twenty-five to eleven. Wolves are two up at half time, but only eight minutes of the forty-minute highlights programme have elapsed. Logic dictates that United will score twice in the second half to force extra time. Logic is sound: United get the two goals and a third in extra time itself to progress to the semi-final. Another important lesson, two down is not the worst score at half time, although the reverse is also true: two up is not the best – two up, frankly, is courting disaster. (See, a mere six months after the victory at Wolves, United squandering a two-goal lead at home to Spurs, John Pratt scoring a goal-of-the-season winner.)*

Hope, not the other team, is the real opponent. Of course this is true whether you are in the ground or not. If you are in the ground, though, you can roar on your support – become the twelfth man (a very, very big twelfth man) – or give vent to your frustration and disapproval, shame the players into greater effort. For the fan following the game at home, often after the event, there is nothing to be done, except perhaps to absent yourself more. Once you have exhausted all your next-week-Gods the only power you have is the power in your legs. You have to know when to walk away, even if it is only to the bathroom. Actually, especially if it is to the bathroom.

Tuesday, 24 April 2007. It is 2–2 in this season's Champions League semi-final first leg at Old Trafford, United and Milan. This is the hardest kind of 2–2 to call: United one up too early – or at least

---

*   The most famous 3–2 in United's history was the 1999 UEFA Champions League semi-final second leg away to Juventus. Level at 1–1 from the first leg (a very late Ryan Giggs goal), United were two down in eleven minutes in Turin. I was watching with my wife in a bar in Montreal where I was reading at the Blue Metropolis Book Festival. (In fact the first thing I had done on arriving in Montreal was identify this as a bar that would be showing the match.) I had never felt more relaxed than I did when that second goal went in, although I did have the double insurance that day of having dreamt the result several months previously. Ask my brother: I told him at a funeral the morning after the dream. And, yes, sadder even than writing about it is dreaming about it. Keane, Yorke and Cole, by the way, the last seven minutes from time. Dream doesn't come close.

not three up soon enough afterwards, as they were in the previous round at home to Roma – pegged back and then overtaken before half time. I have been on my feet in the living room since the equaliser in the fifty-ninth minute. The match is now in the ninety-third. There are seconds remaining. Milan break forward and I make a sudden diagonal run out of the living room and into the downstairs toilet. I could not bear to see them score at this late stage. I am having flashbacks to the 1979 FA Cup Final, the so-called 'Five Minute Final': United losing 2–0, then 2–1, then in the closing minutes drawing level through Belfast's own Sammy McIlroy. In my delirium I ran out of the house meeting my United-supporting neighbour halfway. We hugged, danced around. By the time we got back to our houses it was 3–2 to Arsenal. Alan-fucking-Sunderland.

The best that can happen, I tell myself tonight over the sound of the water churning in the bowl, is that we will end up with the draw that would have seemed a disaster ninety-three minutes and all this beer ago.

I return to the living room in time to see the replay of the ball beating Dida in the Milan goal for Manchester United's winner in front of the Stretford End. The Milan attack foundered almost as soon as I left the room on Ryan Giggs's tackle (oh, behave), Giggs fed Rooney, who shot first time: 3–2 with practically the last kick of the game.

Or at least that's how the commentator explains it. A part of me is disappointed to have missed the goal. The larger part, however, knows for a fact that I did not in the truest sense miss the goal at all. If I had stood my ground Giggs would never have made the tackle and the result would have gone the other way: Kaka, not Rooney, would be lying spread-eagled in celebration on the Old Trafford Turf.

This is not the first time I have conjured a goal from my own bladder.

Wednesday, 7 September 2005, Northern Ireland v England at Windsor Park. I used to be a regular at international home games, through the dark, dark days of the mid- and late 1970s – which were actually light, light days, since even weekday matches had to kick off in the afternoon due to Windsor Park's substandard floodlighting – through the early 1980s World Cup campaigns, and on into the scoreless run that saw us dubbed Northern Ireland Nil. It isn't the results that have kept me away of late, or even the performances, rather the birth of my children and the complications of Wednesday (or any other) evening at 8pm. Now, when I am desperate for a ticket, it is impossible to get hold of one, the Windsor Park capacity having been reduced by about 95 per cent from the wedged-in days when it was possible to go a full ninety minutes on the terracing without your feet once touching the ground. A lecturer friend is over from Japan. He is keen to watch the match. I suggest he come to my house, although I would far rather watch on my own. That is, I would far rather be somewhere else in the house on my own while the TV is on in the living room. After all, I can hardly welcome my friend, set him down with a beer and then run out as soon as England attack, especially given how often England are guaranteed to attack.

For most of the first half they do pretty much nothing else. The only respite is to switch occasionally to the Republic of Ireland v France match on RTÉ, telling myself we are bound to be behind when I turn back. We aren't. This is, for the homebound fan, not good, because worse than England thrashing us would be England sneaking a win just when, insanely and despite all your vigilance and experience, you had begun once again to hope. I hold off until the seventy-third minute, two minutes after the sort of near miss by Northern Ireland that usually precedes the other side scoring. ('I wonder how significant that could be for Lawrie Sanchez's men at the end of the evening?')

'I must just go to the toilet,' I say.

I stay away for as long as seems decent and for as long as will justify another jog down the hallway in injury time if it's still 0–0. When I return to the living room my friend is not there. Or at least I notice his absence from the sofa a fraction of a second before I register his presence on the floor in front of the TV. He is, to be precise, on his knees on the floor in front of the TV: on his knees and with his arms around the TV. There is something in there that he does not want to get out. It is a moment or two more before I realise that the something is a goal for Northern Ireland, another five minutes before I can persuade him the goal is safe, we can sit down again.

We will probably still lose, I say, but at least we scored. I am in the kitchen getting more crisps – slowly opening the bag there, slowly – when the final whistle blows.

My friend from Japan is a Glentoran supporter. He chose them several years back because they seemed to be the Northern Irish team best equipped to progress in Europe (or at least not be effectively out after the first round first leg), because of their non-sectarian policy and because they had the best website. Needless to say he had never seen them play.

'We should go to the Oval when you are next over,' I had said to him last time we met. Unfortunately, Glentoran were not at home while he was in town on this occasion, but three days after the Northern Ireland game we travelled from east to north Belfast to see his team take on Cliftonville at Solitude. I had only ever been there once before, in April 1970, when the ground was chosen as the neutral venue for the Irish Cup Final between Linfield and Ballymena United. Linfield won 2–1, but the match is remembered now mainly for the riot that broke out when fans of both teams clashed with nationalist youths in the streets around the ground. (We were still getting used to the idea in April 1970 that there was no such thing as neutral any more.) For the next three decades Cliftonville had been obliged to play many of their 'home' games away, their supporters escorted through the city by almost the entire RUC Reserve.[*]

By 2005 even so solid a working-class Protestant club as Glentoran can go to Solitude once more, although there is still a lot of security, if not yet by the PSNI inside the ground itself. By dint of not being home fans we have no choice but to sit among the away fans behind one of the goals.

A quarter of an hour before kick-off a steward comes and motions to my friend to follow him. He leads him down on to the pitch where Glentoran are warming up. He invites him to pose for photographs with his favourite player, striker Andy Smith. On Monday morning he is there on the excellent website: 'Your Man from Japan.'

The match is ninety minutes of anti-climax. In the closing stages

---

[*]   The expert on this is Henry McDonald, *Observer* columnist and former member of the Cliftonville 'Red Army'. See *Colours: Ireland from Bomb to Boom* (2005), his 'exercise in time travel' over the last thirty-odd years of life and politics in Northern Ireland.

Glentoran scramble a winner. Andy Smith doesn't score. It's at the far end of the ground from us, so it is several minutes before the identity of the goalscorer reaches us. I have never heard of him and, as I sit here now trying to recall, have quite forgotten him.

A few months later I am in Japan, researching a novel the point of which is increasingly as much a mystery to me as the Glentoran goalscorer's name. Since I am in the vicinity – that is, within a couple of hundred miles – I go to Beppu to see my friend and to talk to his Junior College English students. These are seventeen- and eighteen-year-olds hoping, at most, to teach high school English. They have no particular interest in Northern Ireland, and no particular reason to learn about it. They just happen to have my friend for a teacher. He has a treat for them, for me, a video of his most recent trip to Belfast. The lights are dimmed, the blinds drawn behind my back on Beppu, and there on the wall before me is the Newtownards Road, there is Connswater Shopping Centre, and there eventually (windscreen in between, blacktop, oncoming traffic) is Solitude. Ten minutes into the action – too strong: *proceedings* – I realise there are no edits. We are in real time, not highlights. Untold minutes later my friend's camera swings around and there I am. Except, I am not there at all, any more than I am at this minute in Beppu. I am three hundred miles away, due east of Belfast, at St James's Park, where, a Glentoran fan with a radio has just told me, Manchester United have beaten Newcastle by 1–0.

I do not need to watch.

I am not even sure any more I like to watch.

It is enough to know.

I smile for the camera.

Three Poems

JEAN BLEAKNEY

Imitation

On Looking into Patrick Kavanagh's
'On Reading a Book on Common Wild Flowers'

At first, I thought … good man yourself, Paddy! Grand job!
But that was before my intimacy with prickly sow thistle.
Those blossoms, far from puce, are more in the realms
of dandelion yellow. Questionable too, then,
your heartfelt identification of autumn gentian,
if as you say, clay is the word and clay is the flesh.
Were you having a go, Paddy? Chancing your arm?
Was memory shook? Was the book poorly illustrated?
Or was it viewed in the dim imperative of a Dublin snug?
Ah but sure doesn't all writing generate its own fug.

Let me, likewise, not moralise, who suddenly glimpses
the townland of Poetry's whole motley infantry,
all the way back to Homer and Sappho.
They're swaggering down its laneways and backroads
risking the sheugh for the hedgerow's bounty; quoting,
misquoting, appropriating, misappropriating, muse in tow,
going, as Ledwidge might have said, the road all poets go.

The Yellow Nib, Vol. 3, 2007, pp 83–88
© Jean Bleakney

Evocation

In memory of Margaret Jane Kerr (née Bustard)
1899–1981

The family tell me I curse too much,
forever saying so-and-so or such-and-such
is a bastard. And that it's getting worse
especially my tendency to intersperse
the F-word. I cite the peri-menopause
or that other midlife crisis get-out-clause:
genetics. An aunt or two and Granny Kerr
could always be relied upon to swear.
Ditto the menfolk. Poor Granny: Maggie Jane
driven to distraction and the profane
by arthritis and absentee fodderers
and marriage to one of life's ceilidhers.
An only child, she somehow reared eleven.
Water had to be carried from Lough Melvin
to a homestead fuelled by turf and paraffin oil
and the thin returns of boggy limestone soil.
We'd visit in July, a week-long stay.
Daddy'd be roped in to help with the hay
or dispatched to search for an overdue heifer.
Mostly the sun shone, but whatever the weather
we hung around the house, my sister and I:
townies, at a loss about the how and why.
Half-repulsed, half-scared of hen house, dairy, byre
and penned bull, ready and waiting to sire;
and the flies from the 'duckle' of cowshit
and the twin-holed plank of the outside toilet;
and the grin … the rotten teeth of Tommy Ovens
as he cycled past. We were 'Eddie's ones',
'the cutties'. We'd cross the road to the lake
to look for skimmers or a good straight stick
or hazelnuts, unripe, but creamily sweet;
and try for minnows, but never go in too deep.

Or we'd scan the lane's replenished drainage channel
(hardcore from Carty's quarry) for fossil coral.
Sometimes, we wouldn't even go that far.
We'd take the transistor radio out to the car
and sit there eating our Fry's Dairy Creams.
Shy of passers-by and their alien names
... Dolan, Hughdie, McCordick, Siberry ...
we'd risk the upper lane for wild strawberries,
threaded onto a stalk of grass. But sure
as cat's a beast, our cousins, the McClures
would have stripped the banks, clean as a whistle.
And every evening brought its own epistle
from Uncle Tommy or Granny or Granda
or Norman (home for a month from Canada)
D'ye mind so and so ...(always distant relatives;
the explication worthy of Genesis)
ah he'd be a friend of ...(strange they used 'friend'
for kith and kin). The narrative would wend
... Knocknashangan, Knockareven, Scribbagh
Glennasheever, Correll, Barr of Slattinagh ...
hypnotically, townland by townland,
broken by a query's answer: *Ah he's doin' grand.*
And whether they were angry or not,
every man jack of them seemed to shout
and everything was *wild* or *fierce* or *ojus.*
(By some kind of inverse extravagance,
whoever'd be dying would be *not too great.*)
And there'd be somebody about to speculate
on land or a horse or a Massey Ferguson;
and always someone to say *There'll be ructions*
– announced with a tilt of the head or a knowing shrug
or an emphatically raised striped mug
or shot glass; almost as if they were willing it.
The wooden kitchen chairs were a hard sit,
especially for youngsters. Grandfather Kerr
sat by the range in an old leather armchair.
Tea and an egg, and warfarin, for fear of clots,

and pills 'for his water' and Epsom salts
– his morning ritual as, stroke by stroke,
he slurred and slowed, though still fit to smoke.
And there he'd sit, all ears for 'company'
though deaf to the lamentations of Granny.
He'd offer the 'childer' a suck of his pipe
if it was nearly out. Granny would snipe
Quit that, Willie! And you learned to sit
out of range of the hook of his walking stick.
The rheumier the eyes, the lower the felt hat,
the quieter he'd be. Hard to imagine that,
for his way with beasts, though with slim recompense,
he'd been unoffical 'vit' to half the county. (Hence
words like glanders and warbles and 'the staggers'
that still bubbled up in my Customs Man father
who, like his father before him, had the wherewithal,
the *grá*, to saw … illicitly … the horns off cattle.)
On wet days, no longer able to pretend
interest in a yellowed *People's Friend*,
we'd explore the parlour's riches: old photos
and Daddy's Far Eastern wartime mementoes
(a model junk; a ship in a light bulb).
But a change in the tone of the kitchen hubbub
would bring us back. Granny'd be in a lather
at the mention of some or other 'bother'.
Her sweetly sheepish smile could suddenly switch:
Bad cess to him, she'd say, or *man he's a bitch*
or *man he's a hoor*. Though half the time
it was *man oh man oh man oh man* she'd rhyme,
running her sore hands over sore hips
with a low whistle of pain through pursed lips.
Addressing no one in particular, she'd say
Well it wouldn't do to vex me this day
as she heeled a pot of blues into the colander
or knuckled floury dough at the open dresser.
But she'd loved to read; took a book to bed
some afternoons, the plait loosed from her head.

The glass-fronted bookcase behind her bedroom door
was our favourite place. We'd hunker on the floor
when the coast was clear and scan the worm-holed spines
… westerns, Defoes, and green and cream Penguins
alongside a *Tales from the Holy Land*
(a Sunday School Prize), some Mills & Boons and,
I swear to God, her hardback *Dr No*.
And even though that's nearly forty years ago,
despite the sliceable tensions, the chair,
the flies, the smoke-blue/word-blue air,
sometimes I wish … sometimes I think I'm back there.

Recuperation

Whether to put the tulips or the lilies
centre-table is the day's dilemma.
Whether to consolidate … except

tulips are tulips. Too self-possessed
to cohabit. The lilies were there first.
They're already bunched: oriental

with still-in-bud *longiflorum*.
Should the new usurp? Darlings,
I've come over all Mrs Dalloway;

I'm dreamily Virginia-tinged in this
post-anaesthesia lassitude. Day 4:
even flower placement defeats me.

It's as if my brain's shrink-wrapped;
that or I'm sitting on its doorstep
waiting for somebody else's key.

See how cut tulips right themselves
taking their bearings less
from light than from gravity.

Nine Poems after Yannis Ritsos

DAVID HARSENT

The Writing Table

Remember when you wrote a poem a day
at this old table? Now it's full of worm-holes,
of bullet-holes. The night-wind plays it like a flute.

Sometimes, just before dawn, Urania descends.
She sets her white gloves down on that same table,
her white handbag, her starry bangles,
and lies beside you while you sleep. Or else pretend to sleep.

The Yellow Nib, Vol. 3, 2007, pp 89–98

In Secret

They were calling across the water ... calling a name.
Once he was sure it was his, he ran and hid.
An ocean-going liner slipped out of the harbour
all lights blazing; on the upper deck a woman
wearing a picture hat. It blocked his view
of the dark tower, the moon, the waiting scaffold.

from Hints

That ancient coin in your pocket ... had you forgotten?
Your finger traces the young god's nakedness.

*

A man standing in darkness smiles a secret smile ...
Is that because he can see in the dark? Maybe; or maybe
because he can see the dark.

*

The sunflowers almost hide the wall, the wall
hides the road completely. Beyond that you've got houses,
trees, hills, certain wrongdoings ... In the heat of the day,
men from the lumberyard go down to take a piss.
At night the dead come out to whitewash the wall.

*

Want to know what's truly important (he asked) about art?
I'll tell you. It's everything you leave out, whether or not
you mean to: like that knife in the basket there, hidden
under the grapes. Under the purple grapes.

*

No gift of words all year ... Even so, his lamp
burns all night
in case a poem should stumble in.

*

He walked away from the market-place, the babble,
the second-hand fridges, the bowls and baskets,
'fresh produce' on the turn or else gone over ...
He went into his house, he closed his door, he sat in his chair,
he sharpened his pencil (slowly, carefully) and wept.

*

Given a last request, they asked
for a paper bag apiece which, somehow, someone found,
whereupon they blew them up and, turning, burst
the bags against the wall, then dropped like stones.

Women

Our women are distant; their sheets smell of goodnight.
They put bread on the table as a token of themselves.
It's then that we finally see we were at fault; we jump up saying,
'Look, you've done too much, take it easy, I'll light the lamp.'

She turns away with the striking of the match,
walking towards the kitchen, her face in shadow, her back
bent under the weight of so many dead –
those you both loved, those she loved, those
you alone loved … yes … and your death also.

Listen: the bare boards creaking where she goes.
Listen: the dishes weeping in the dishrack.
Listen: the train taking soldiers to the front.

In the Rain

He walks in the rain ... no hurry ...
The railings glisten; the trees
are black, with a faint red underblush;
there's an old bus-tyre in the sheep-pen.

The blue house looks much bluer in this light.

It's all a means to make nothing
less than it was. Rockfall. A clenched fist.
In the river, an empty envelope; perhaps
your name and address are on the other side.

Morning

She threw back the shutters and spread
the bedsheets on the windowsill.
It was broad day. A bird stared back at her.

'I'm alone, I'm alive ...'

She stood in front of the mirror.
'This, too, is a window. If I jump,
I'll fall into my own arms.'

On Colour

Red mountain. Green sea. Yellow sky.
And the earth is blue.

A bird. A leaf.
And perched between them, death.

Suddenly

A quiet night, so quiet, so still, and you
have stopped waiting. And then, somehow,
his touch on your face, electric, as if …

He'll come. Though all at once
a wind is getting up, the shutters are banging,
and the sound of the sea is a distant, drowning voice.

1972

Each night, gunfire. Come dawn, a sudden silence.
Blank walls, floors scrubbed clean, chairs arranged just so.

Think of a door, and beyond it a door,
and another door beyond that, the spaces between
crammed with the kind of cotton-waste they use
to fill the mouths of the starving or the dead ...

Our heroes are small men, pasty-faced and fat.

Her Britannic Majesty

IAN SANSOM

Gin. That was my drink. My tipple, as they say. The old juniper berry. Gin and tonic with a slice of lemon. Good old English drink. Nice and clear and strong.

I was never much of a one for the beer. And wine, no. Definitely not. Wine I never really bothered with at all. It was always the gin, given a choice. I always liked a drop of gin.

Not that I'm a heavy drinker. Despite what was said.

I can probably remember the first time a drop of alcohol passed my lips. Father was back from the war. We were having some sort of a party. I must have been, what, seven or eight? The parties were different then, in those days. Not like they are now. Sing-song sort of parties, they were: a knees-up, that's what we'd have called it.

Anyway, rum, it was, the alcohol. He'd brought back a bottle of rum, Dad; he was in the navy. That's what they drank, in the navy. A bottle of rum to warm your tum, isn't it. And the rum was on the table in the kitchenette. And there was a banana as well. I can see it now, the banana. I'd never seen a real banana before. I'd only seen pictures, in the *Picture Post*, I think it was. I don't know where he'd got the banana – won it, probably.

The piano was in the parlour. Everyone seemed to know how to play the piano in those days. It was just something you did – tinkling the old ivories. You didn't have to learn; no one had lessons or anything. And if you couldn't play the piano you were expected to do a turn. My aunt Jessie, she had a lovely singing voice – she'd always do a few songs. Music hall, she did. When she'd had a few, she'd hitch up her skirts.

And then there was my uncle Bert. He could juggle. Three balls. He wasn't bad. Paper-tearing he did as well – he could make a ladder. And Ernie, my other uncle, Ernie, he played mouth-organ. He said he'd taken it from a dead German soldier. It was certainly, you know, what's the word, very mournful the way he played it. Very sad. He kept it by his bed right up until he died. Even when he was in the hospital he had that mouth-organ. He kept it next to his false teeth. I visited him once, with Mother. He was up at St Thomas's; he used to play the mouth-organ for the old folks and the nurses.

'Cheer 'em up a bit,' he used to say. He'd do the Last Post.

And anyway, Mother it was who played the piano. Lovely long fingers, she had.

'She's got a full octave stretch,' Father used to say.

I can remember it as clear as if it were yesterday, walking into the parlour and Mother sitting there playing the piano, and my aunt Jessie singing, and Ernie with his mouth-organ, and Bert with a paper ladder, and my father drinking this rum from our china cups, and I was sick, right there on the rug, in front of everybody. It was the combination of the rum and the banana, I suppose.

Not a good mix, rum and banana.

He took his belt to me for that. Waited till everyone had gone, mind. Buckle-end he used, on us boys. The girls, he only used the leather on the girls. That seemed fair to me at the time. That was just what happened. That was before all this – what do you call it – political correctness.

He used to keep it warming by the fire, his belt. He called it Little Jack-a-Dandy. I don't know why. Maybe it was a navy thing.

'D'you want me to get Little Jack-a-Dandy?' I can remember him shouting, when he was getting angry. 'Do you? D'you want me to get Little Jack-a-Dandy?'

And then if he did, if he did lose his temper, he'd say to one of us, 'Get me Little Jack-a-Dandy.' And one of us would go and get it.

The piano in the parlour, that went in the end, of course, like everything else, because of Father. His only turn was a three-card trick. He couldn't do anything else. He was a gambler. Loved the cards. And the horses. And the dogs. Anything you could put a bet on.

He wasn't too bad before the war, Mother always said, but after the war, that was it. I don't know what he thought. Maybe he was just glad to be back. Glad to be alive, and what have you. He used to meet up with his cronies at the weekends – that's what Mother used to call them, cronies. You don't hear people say that now, 'cronies'. That's what she called them though. First the pub, and then they'd go back to someone's house for a few more drinks, and then it'd be a few hands of cards and in the end he lost everything. To his friends. Or so-called friends. Cronies – that's the word, isn't it.

There was a pearl necklace that was Gran's. That went. Mother, she used to talk about that necklace for years after. I don't know if it was pawned or what, or if it just changed hands there and then. It just disappeared; went; gone.

And once he'd lost everything and there was nothing left for him to lose, *he* went. That was all that was left. Upped, walked out the door and didn't come back.

I always thought he'd be back. As a child, you don't think that anyone can just leave. You don't think it's possible, just to leave; I didn't know what it meant, leaving. I thought when you left you always had to come back. That's how I thought as a child.

We had to move out of the house, of course. It was sort of a maisonette – it wasn't bad. Streatham, it was. Mother couldn't pay the rent once he'd gone. We couldn't ever pay the rent after that, so we didn't have any choice, we'd just up sticks and off we'd go, right there and then, in the middle of the night. Midnight flit, isn't it. I was the eldest, so I used to help Mother pack up and get the others ready. People now, of course, they have so much, so many – what do you call them? – possessions, that's it, possessions and what have you, they couldn't do that now. But we used to do it all the time, just up sticks. Get up, pack up, and quick out through the streets before anyone saw us, and start all over again somewhere else. Midnight flit. We were like gypsies. Nowhere to lay our heads, and what have you.

I was always worried he might return one day and not be able to find us. So I used to write these little notes on these little pieces of paper, little scraps, you know, whatever I could find, and I'd roll 'em up and stuff 'em between the cracks in the floorboards, or between the skirting and the wall. We've had to leave, I'd say. We're going to Battersea, or wherever, wherever it was I'd picked up we were going from Mother, and I'd draw a little map for him.

He never found them, of course.

'He'll find us,' mother used to say, 'if he wants to find us.'

And one day he did.

Mother had him back, of course. The girls didn't want him back. Or my brothers. I didn't mind though. I was fifteen by that time, or sixteen I think it was. And anyway he was like an old man by then. He looked like an old man. He'd grown this beard – because he'd been a navy man, I suppose.

He slept in the front room, on the little settee, where we'd ended up, which was in Battersea, in the old Andrews buildings there, by the warehouse. They're not there anymore, of course, the buildings. They knocked them down. I don't know. Nineteen-sixties, was it?

He was only ever allowed to sleep in the front room, Father. Mother wouldn't have him in the bed. She'd had him back, but that was as far as she'd go, I suppose. He slept on the settee, fully clothed with an old blanket over him, this sort of red blanket – bright red, it was – that he rolled up every morning and kept in this little old suitcase. Little blue suitcase. He was more like a guest than a dad, when he came back. He was like a stranger, you know, in his own house.

He never slept properly, mind. He kept navy hours, is what he said. Sometimes, if I was awake, I'd hear him moving around in there, in the front room. It was a funny noise, him being so close, not knowing what he was doing. He was in and out of work, didn't read or anything and there was no television in those days – we didn't have a wireless even – so I never knew what he was doing in there, early in the morning. Shuffling around. Breathing. He was thinking, I expect. You don't really understand that until you're a bit older yourself.

It was sad really. Mother wouldn't allow him to do anything round the house. He wasn't allowed to touch anything. He wasn't allowed to touch us. We were too big by that time anyway, but if there was a problem Mother would get Bert to help her out, or Ernie. I suppose she was punishing him, really. She didn't want him to think he was the man of the house anymore, wasn't it, after what he'd done, leaving us. She let him make his porridge at the weekends, but that was about it. Little dash of rum in the porridge. He was drinking all day then, you see. Alcoholic now they'd call him, wouldn't they. I never touched it, the porridge; I'd have gone hungry rather than eat his porridge. I'd got very bitter about him leaving us. Deserting his family and that. I thought that was . . . what? Unforgivable. I thought you had to stay.

I was working at that time, my first job, at the old Mazawattee Tea Company, down by the Grand Regent Canal. Sweeping up is what I was doing. I don't know what I was paid, I can't remember, about twelve shillings a week. Maybe not as much. That was a long time ago. I saved up and bought a second-hand bike. No gears or anything, but a nice bike, you know. It wasn't bad. On Sundays I used to cycle all about, exploring. I used to go the library on Poplar High Street, where they had this map, A to Z type of thing I suppose it was, except in this nice sort of leather volume, and I'd have a look at it, and I'd plan my route and off I went. If you got lost in those days you could just stop and ask a policeman, it wasn't all these motorways. I went out as far as Epping a couple of times, Epping Forest. Lovely out there it was – no policemen out there – the freedom of it, you know. Fresh air. You'd almost think you could do anything, out on a bike – go anywhere, do anything. You'd have all these feelings, out on the bike. You'd take these huge breaths. Like the world was your oyster.

That's how I met Elizabeth, out on the bike. That was my wife; Lizzie we called her. I was out cycling one Sunday, just setting off, going down Poplar High Street, and there was some stones or some glass or something in the road up ahead, and Lizzie, she stepped out into the road, and flagged me down, to warn me like. She was like that, very ... what's-it-called? Civic-minded, isn't it? Civic-minded. A civic-minded sort of person, she was. Very good-hearted. Organised. Lovely looking as well – red hair, she had. She had some Irish in her. Fiery, you know.

She saved me from getting a puncture, so I started cycling that way every Sunday. The churches all had afternoon services then, I think it was, and she'd be on her way to church and I'd cycle past and ring my bell and wave and then eventually I used to get off the bike, and wheel it along, talking to her, whatever it is you talk about. And then she got us organised and we got married, and had the children.

And that was it.

And then she had the accident.

She worked up in town, Lizzie, selling handkerchiefs. In Selfridges, mind you, none of your old rubbish. She'd had elocution lessons, when she was little. Her mum, you see, she was, what do you call it? Forward-thinking, isn't it. There were three of them in those days on the handkerchief counter, just selling the handkerchiefs. Hard to credit now, isn't it. She loved that job. She knew all about handkerchiefs, all the different linens and the embroidery. She used to get the bus up there. She used to look lovely in her uniform. I went in to see her once, when she was working. There was a shut-down at the yard, so I had a free afternoon and I put on my suit, and went up there to Selfridges just to see her. Walked right in – I'd never been to Selfridges before. I didn't go up to the counter. I didn't want to embarrass her. She didn't see me. I just stood there, watching her, watching her talking to the customers, like, watching her smiling. It was strange. It was a strange feeling.

Then it wasn't long after that, when she was getting off the bus and she fell and banged her head.

She was in this place up at Queen's Square and at first the doctors said there was nothing they could do for her. It was an aneurysm, they said. *Aneurysm*, that's what they said. But the technology was changing. She might be, one day, not normal, they said, but, you know, better.

So she came home, and she was at home with us for years, waiting to get better.

She didn't get better.

In the end she had go back into the hospital, permanently like. I suppose that's when I was a single parent. When she was in the house it was still like we were together as a family, even though she wasn't really there – having to feed her, and bathe her and what have you. But then when she went in the hospital, when she'd gone … It got a bit lonely. That was when I was a single parent really, except no one would have thought of calling me a single parent in those days. There was no such thing as single parents then. You were a widower, or whatever.

Except of course Lizzie wasn't dead.

Anyway, there was our little boy and girl to look after. My mother, she was gone by then, and the children, I felt bad for them. Not having a mother, not really. They were too young to understand. So it was difficult. To them their idea of a mother was this woman who was lying in bed, being fed, you know, and we had to mash up all her food and everything.

Richard, our boy, he found it the hardest. Not to have a mother, that's hard on a boy. But there wasn't anything I could do about it. I just did my best. Keep the family together, just working and that, you know.

I ended up as foreman, at work, in the end. Sand and gravel it was; different yards, here and there. For the concrete, like. We were called British and Commonwealth Aggregates when I started. That's the word for it – aggregates. Then it was just British Aggregates, and then British and European Aggregates. Now it's Euromix. So that tells you a story, doesn't it, of how times have changed.

I was quite proud of that little job; wasn't a bad little job. You say concrete to people these days, of course, and it's like a dirty word. People forget what concrete was after the war. Concrete was the future, after the war.

Then the first grandchild. That was something. Great, that was. Anne – that's our boy Richard, his wife – she's a lovely girl, really. Lizzie would have liked her. Little bit of, you know, spark about her.

He was at the birth, Richard. That's what happens these days. In my day it was all different; you were just in the way; they wanted you out of the way.

Anyway, Sophie. That's what they called her. Little beauty she was. Took after the other side more than our side. Little button nose.

Blonde hair. Lovely looking. She wasn't well at first. She was on the antibiotics. But that was soon cleared up.

I couldn't get over her, when she was born. It was like magic.

I didn't get to see them much. They're just outside Oxford – nice place – that's where Anne's parents are. It's not that far, Oxford, couple of hours on the motorway, but, you know …

We'd had the contract for the motorway. British and Commonwealth Aggregates. We done all the motorways. That's the beauty of concrete. You feel as though you're a part of the whole thing, you see. Because it's – what's the word? Ubiquitous, isn't it. Ubiquitous. You could feel a part of it.

I never missed a birthday. I was always there for the birthdays.

Her third birthday; I couldn't believe it. Three. I spent ages shopping for all the presents. I went up into town for the day, into Hamleys. Lovely jigsaw I got her. And this little hobby-horse. Beautiful. You're allowed to spoil them, aren't you, your grandchildren. You can't do it with your own, of course, you have to teach your own to be whatever it is … self-reliant. Not greedy and what have you. Not to take anything for granted. But with your grandchildren you can spoil them rotten.

She loved those presents.

She always says the same when she sees me. 'Grandad, Grandad, Grandad,' she says, and she dances this little sort of dance, you know. Gives me a big hug. Lovely little girl.

I'd dandle her on my knee. Dandle – that's another word you don't hear people using much these days. *Dandle*.

She loved a cuddle though. Cuddles weren't so important in the old days. My old mum and dad, you know, they weren't great cuddlers.

It was a little birthday tea she was having. Anne's parents were there. They're nice people. He's in management. Social services. She's a social worker, her mother.

We had birthday cake.

He was doing the honours, Anne's father.

'Let's have a little celebration,' he said. Champagne, he'd brought. I hadn't thought of that. I never really liked the taste of champagne. I had a gin and tonic.

And then another one.

'Dad,' Richard said, 'You're driving.'

I knew I was driving. A couple of drinks, though. People get very fussed up about things these days. Smoking and what have you. Everyone used to smoke before. And have a drink. At work, in the old days, everyone would have a few drinks every lunchtime. Managers as well, like. Didn't seem to be a problem then.

I never really agreed with all that, being told you had to wear a seatbelt and you couldn't drink and drive. I was Labour when I was younger.

'One gin and tonic,' I said.

'Two,' Richard said.

'Well, two,' I said. 'It's hardly going to kill me, is it.'

I've never been a big drinker. That's the irony of it really. We even had Methodists in the family – Ernie, he went Methodist. Teetotallers, aren't they, Methodists.

After the party, I didn't want to get in the way. You know. I thought I'd leave them to it.

So I kissed them goodbye.

Kissed little Sophie goodbye.

'Bye bye, Grandad,' she said.

'Bye bye, Princess,' I said.

What happened next.

I know I started up the car. Started reversing. I know I checked my mirror. I've always been a careful sort of driver – mirror, signal, manoeuvre.

But.

Didn't see her.

It was my fault. There's no getting away from that.

Police investigation. Quite right. Had to get to the bottom of it. They were quite right. Courts and that.

After, I spoke to Richard just the once. On the phone, like. He asked me not to get in contact any more. Quite right.

Quite right.

The house has been getting too much for me anyway. I was only living in one room in the end. I'd sort of – what's-it-called – retreated, you know. Room to room. Out of the upstairs first. I wasn't sleeping anyway.

And then eventually downstairs. Couldn't see any point in the kitchen – I wasn't cooking. So I brought the microwave into the living room. Had the telly in there, couple of blankets, one of those, you know, little convector heaters. That was fine. I didn't go out much anyway. Just food and bills. And in the end I just decided to get rid of everything. Rang up a fella from the paper.

He came round with a clipboard, went from room to room.

'Well,' he said, 'there's not much of any value.'

He was only doing his job. Beating me down, like. I don't blame him. He had a photocopied sheet, and he'd ticked off all these things. Standard lamp. Footstool. Mirrors. Tables. Chairs. Bedside cabinets. Wardrobes. Television. Hi-fi. There was a space for Miscellaneous. He'd written in 'coal box', and 'typewriter' – that was Lizzie's, the typewriter.

He showed it to me, the list. Guess how much?

For all that. What do you call it? Booty – that's it. Booty of a lifetime. How much?

Five hundred pounds. He didn't say five hundred pounds. He just indicated the figure on his clipboard.

I signed and they collected that afternoon. Couldn't let me change my mind, I suppose. Not that I would have changed my mind.

It felt a lot better, getting the house cleared. It was a weight off my mind. Richard wouldn't have been wanting it anyway, all my old junk.

I forgot about the shed though. I had to get my neighbour round for the tools.

'Are you sure about this?' he said.

'Oh yes,' I said, 'I'm too old for this game.'

Once the tools and all the other – what's it? paraphernalia – were gone there wasn't that much left.

Only the bike. It was the bike that gave me the idea.

I kept on cycling when we were first married. But once we got the car and what with Lizzie and the children and what have you, the bike languished – that's the word. Languished. I occasionally took it out for a ride in the summer, but that was it.

It's a nice bike. Gears and everything. I can still remember buying that bike, what, forty years ago now? Something like that. Gillespie's, it was. He had a shop, Mr Gillespie. Long gone now, of course. He went into it all with me, the size and weight of the frame and that. It was like having a suit measured. It was always my ambition to have a suit made for me, in Savile Row.

It wasn't in bad nick, all things considered. I gave it a bit of a clean, sponged it down, scraped off some of the rust on the wheel rims. Got my pacamac in the saddlebag.

I hadn't planned anything really. I just got on, and started riding. Put the key under the flowerpot, turned off the lights, shut the back gate, and left. It was good to get the fresh air in my lungs.

I'd only got to the bottom of the road when I remembered the dog.

I couldn't have left him on his own. I can remember him as a puppy, putting all the paper down to train him.

Buried him in his basket.

Going down with the ship and all that.

They dipped the cranes as Churchill went by.

And then I got back on the bike, and went.

You see things when you're out riding that you wouldn't notice otherwise – just, you know, things. It's all changed a lot.

If I'd thought about it a bit more I probably wouldn't have left when I did. Rush hour starting, all the cars. You forget how busy it gets. School run and that. But after an hour I was surprised. You can cover a lot of ground in an hour.

I remember saying to the children, when they were young, learning to ride the bike, 'You control the bike. The bike doesn't control you. You're in charge,' I would say. But.

Three and a half hours, it took – the old knees getting a bit creaky and stiff at the end there, and the calf-muscles, that's where it gets you. But. Made it. What is it they say? Nowhere in the UK more than seventy miles from the sea, isn't it?

And it is a sight.

I can't say when I saw the sea …

I don't know. Everything seems to happen in a big rush, doesn't it? Life, it's a big rush, isn't it? What's the word for it? Inexplicable, isn't it. Inexplicable rush. And that becomes your life, you see. No time for rest or what-do-you-call-it. Reflection.

The bike up against the wall there. Just dropped down onto the pebbles. Shoes off. Keeping the clothes on, mind. You know, in case there's people about. Chilly sort of evening.

We came here when the children were little. Similar, anyway. There was a Punch and Judy man. Punch and Judy, and the baby, and the what's it – policeman, and the crocodile. He wouldn't come out, Punch. All the children had to shout.

There we are.

Emptied out my pockets. Few pounds; the old cash machine card. And the passport. I don't know. I thought I should bring the passport.

It is cold. Cold and grey. But just then for a moment, just when I put my head under, everything is absolutely clear.

Three Poems

MEDBH McGUCKIAN

The Plumrose Anemone

The lime coral alters and recrystallises, slipping
Between. In the afternoon yellow,
A breastsling is paired by its shadow.

Purple wreathwort twists its old leaf
In her ovary, or a leaf about to be old,
Gifted with a flower. She keeps to the corners
Of her counterpane, her bed set
With plates and dishes. Her veins are parallel
Like pillars of books, her skirt is stretched out
At the hips where her canvas petticoat
Gapes open. She wears a foul mob
Over the perfect, glossy folds of her hair,
Thus gambling with her grace.

At the wind-rounded hour of low water,
We drape her with bright red fabric
Most gratefully fragrant. The currach
Sleeps on its back in the grass,
The curve of its belly upturned like a star
Washed ashore, by the abolition of all metaphor.

Woman Examining
Her Breasts in a Mirror

Why do I always return to the sunken road
Through corroded hills where the moon entered
The double-shuttered windows? Who would forbid
Light being taken from neighbouring light?

Keep far away slender headboards
And you long borders who cover half the feet.
He is reading with his right finger a stretched breast
The new muse has unwoven.

Overflow of flowers in the wilder bit of the garden.
He teaches by what juices kisses disappear
From the holy see of the body
Where swallows now are seldom seen singly.

Around the foreshore a straggling absence
Of swastika banners on church steeples:
The sea is splashed by stars and rented
Nailspaces along alleyways.

The war-scalloped square is attacked
By brightness. The rain-gathering
Uplands breathe uninterrupted
Views of Government House.

Kaluza's Law

The lake, with its almost healed scar,
In its blue-grey withdrawal is all arms,
Badge of white on the thigh. A foggy day
Turns white linen brown and faintly browns
The meagre winter flowers, displaying
This degree of wear and tear, a quality of decay
In the sky.

A half-imaginary Irish saint
Is stepping after the sybil in praise of moss
And its unvarying, thin green notebooks
Where the letters of her heather coiffure are lost
Through eyeskip. Spry enough,
The blackish flowers in their bowlful of time,
With its inlay of lakes.

An older angel protrudes from the blue
Shadow of a church, from pew ends with poppies,
Caretaker of seven sparsely feathered wings.
The arrowshaft hastens with its feather gear,
The flukes on the arrowhead bend the sedge
Double out on the heath.

Then the slow chamfering of a stone's edge
By blown sandgrains, while the still-fluttering
Goatmoth settles for stillness.

A Poem and Three Songs

PAUL MULDOON

A Hare at Aldergrove

A hare standing up at last on his own two feet
in the blasted grass by the runway may trace his lineage to the great
assembly of hares that, in the face of what might well have looked like defeat,
would, in 1963 or so, migrate
here from the abandoned airfield at Nutt's Corner, not long after
    Marilyn Monroe
overflowed from her body-stocking
in *Something's Got to Give*. These hares have themselves so long been
    given to row
against the flood that when a King
of the Hares has tried to ban bare knuckle fighting, so wont
are they to grumble and gripe
about what will be acceptable and what won't
they've barely noticed that the time is ripe
for them to shake off the din
of a pack of hounds that has caught their scent
and take in that enormity just as I've taken in
how my own DNA is 87 per cent European and East Asian 13 per cent.
So accustomed had they now grown
to a low-level human hum that, despite the almost weekly atrocity
in which they'd lost one of their own
to a wheeled blade, they followed the herd towards this eternal city

The Yellow Nib, Vol. 3, 2007, pp 114–121

as if they'd had a collective change of heart.
My own heart swells now as I watch him nibble on a shoot
of blaeberry or heather while smoothing out a chart
by which he might somehow divine if our Newark-bound 757 will one
    day overshoot
the runway about which there so often swirled
rumours of Messerschmitts.
Clapper-lugged, cleft-lipped, he looks for all the world
as if he might never again put up his mitts
despite the fact that he, too, shares a Y chromosome
with Niall of the Nine Hostages,
never again allow his Om
to widen and deepen by such easy stages,
never relaunch his campaign as melanoma has relaunched its campaign
in a friend I once dated,
her pain rising above the collective pain
with which we've been inundated
as this one or that has launched an attack
to the slogan of 'Brits Out' or 'Not an Inch'
or a dull ack-ack
starting up in the vicinity of Ballynahinch,
looking for all the world as if he might never again get into a fluster
over his own entrails,
never again meet lustre with lustre
in the eye of my dying friend, never establish what truly ails
another woman with a flesh wound
found limping where a hare has only just been shot, never again bewitch
the milk in the churn, never swoon as we swooned
when Marilyn's white halter-top dress blew up in *The Seven Year Itch*,
in a flap now only as to whether
we should continue to tough it out till
something better comes along or settle for this salad of blaeberry
    and heather
and a hint of common tormentil.

Owls to Athens

I got how the McGuffin just kickstarts the plot
You're bringing owls to Athens
giving me what I've got
I know she slept with Kevin at that last trade show
You're bringing owls to Athens
telling me what I know

I got how I'd told her often I would change my spots
You're bringing owls to Athens
giving me what I've got
I know how Jane Smith-Hyphen came as quite a blow
You're bringing owls to Athens
telling me what I know

I got how her sense of grievance was bought as a job-lot
You're bringing owls to Athens
giving me what I've got
I know she kinda stiffens when we meet at the Mirabeau
You're bringing owls to Athens
telling me what I know

I got how *Unforgiven* gave Clint another shot
You're bringing owls to Athens
giving me what I've got
I know I'm still ravenous though I've eaten so much crow
You're bringing owls to Athens
telling me what I know

I got how *Kingdom of Heaven* did it for Ridley Scott
You're bringing owls to Athens
giving me what I've got
I know we're even-steven our ratings are so low
You're bringing owls to Athens
telling me what I know

I got how Jane Smith-Hyphen kinda stirred the pot
You're bringing owls to Athens
giving me what I've got
I know she too slept with Kevin at that last trade show
You're bringing owls to Athens
telling me what I know

Good as it Gets

Like Holden Caulfield in spotting phonies
or Stephen Sondheim in winning Tonys
you're a sort of pioneer
like Davy Crockett in knowing trails
or Salome in throwing veils
over what had been quite clear

though you've not set out
to assuage my doubt
it was obvious from the outset
you're just about as good as it gets

like Piggy now his glasses were broken
or Ol' Blue Eyes back in Hoboken
with the local racketeers
like Al Capone in redeeming rum
or Marilyn in seeming dumb
you're improving with the years

though you don't quite chime
with my sense of time
and your diary's not a Letts
you're just about as good as it gets

I fell in love with you on the courts
when you showed me your forehand shot
when I teased you about contact sports
and you gave just as good as you got

like Hans Andersen in 'The Ugly Duckling'
or Errol Flynn in his swashbuckling
and swinging from chandeliers
like Robin Hood in righting wrongs
or Ira Gershwin in writing songs
you're pretty much without peer

though you still don't rub
shoulders with me at the club
and you're not listed in Debrett's
you're still just about as good as it gets

Resistance

Until break of day
it was touch and go
but Juliet gave way
to Romeo
a leader in her field
a cold war strategist
Isolde would yield
to Tristan's tryst

your mother was in the resistance
the Gestapo asking questions
the SS at the door
Now we've gone underground
you may have found
you can't resist me much more

in a purple tent
on the Zuider Zee
Cleopatra would relent
to Antony
once just good friends
in the green wood
Marian would bend
to Robin Hood

your mother was in the resistance
the Gestapo asking questions
the SS at the door
now we've gone underground
you may have found
you can't resist me much more

these seventeen miles
of corridors
under the Pentagon
I thought I saw you smile
at the perimeter guard
his nametag read Von Braun

those seventeen miles
of corridors
under the Pentagon
if we spend a while
in close quarters
maybe you'll fall upon

your knee and kiss the rod
as the goddess of the chase
might submit to a greek god
with a good grace
or having told her beads
in the convent yard
Héloïse would cede
to Abelard

your mother was in the resistance
the Gestapo asking questions
the SS at the door
now we've gone underground
you may have found
you can't resist me much more

Notes on Contributors

CHRIS AGEE was born in 1956 in San Francisco and grew up in Massachusetts, New York and Rhode Island. He has lived in Ireland since 1979. He is the author of two collections of poems, *In the New Hampshire Woods* (1992) and *First Light* (2003), and editor of *Scar on the Stone: Contemporary Poetry from Bosnia* (1998) and *Unfinished Ireland: Essays on Hubert Butler* (2003). He teaches at the Open University and edits *Irish Pages*, a journal of contemporary writing.

JEAN BLEAKNEY was born in Newry, County Down, and now lives in Belfast, where she works in a garden centre. She was commissioned to design the garden at the Seamus Heaney Centre for Poetry. She has published two collections of poetry, *The Ripple Tank Experiment* (1999) and *The Poet's Ivy* (2003), and is currently working on a third.

DAVID BURLEIGH grew up in Portrush, and lives in Tokyo. He teaches at Ferris University in Yokohama. *A Hidden Pond* (Kadokawa Shoten), an anthology of modern haiku that he co-translated with Kōko Katō, received Best Translation Award from the Haiku Society of America for 1997, and a revised edition appeared in 2003. He has also edited *Helen Waddell's Writings from Japan* (2005).

ANDREW ELLIOTT lives in Glasgow. His second collection of poetry, *Lung Soup*, will be published by Blackstaff Press in spring 2008.

LEONTIA FLYNN was born in 1974 in County Down, and her first collection of poems, *These Days*, was published in 2004 by Jonathan Cape. It won the Forward Prize for Best First Collection and was short-listed for the Whitbread Prize. She is a Research Fellow at the Seamus Heaney Centre for Poetry at Queen's, where she is re-working her Ph.D. thesis on Medbh McGuckian, and working on a second poetry collection.

DAVID HARSENT's *Legion* won the Forward Prize for the Best Collection 2005 and was short-listed for both the T.S. Eliot and Whitbread awards. His work in music theatre has been performed at the Royal Opera House, the Concertgebouw, Carnegie Hall and the Proms. A new opera, *The Minotaur*, a collaboration with Harrison Birtwistle, will open at the ROH in 2008. His *Selected Poems* was published by Faber & Faber in 2007.

TOBY LITT was born in 1968. He is the author of *Adventures in Capitalism* (1996; new edition 2003), *Beatniks* (1997; new edition 2004), *Corpsing* (2000), *deadkidsongs* (2001), *Exhibitionism* (2002; new edition 2003), *Finding Myself* (2003, new edition 2004), *Ghost Story* (2004) and *Hospital* (2007). His new novel, *I Play the Drums in a Band Called Okay*, will be published in March 2008. He is a Granta Best of Young British Novelist. His website is www.tobylitt.com.

MEDBH McGUCKIAN is the author of twelve collections of poetry. Her most recent collection, *The Currach Requires No Harbours* (2006), was short-listed for the Irish Times Poetry Now Award. Her other awards include the Rooney Prize for Irish Literature (1982), the Alice Hunt Bartlett Award (1983) and the Cheltenham Prize (1989) and the Forward Prize for Best Single Poem (2002). She is currently a Creative Writing Fellow at the Seamus Heaney Centre for Poetry.

MARTIN MOONEY's first collection, *Grub*, won the 1994 Brendan Behan Memorial Prize. His other collections are *Rasputin and His Children* (2000) and *Blue Lamp Disco* (2004). He is currently working on his first novel.

SINEAD MORRISSEY has published three collections of poetry: *There Was Fire in Vancouver* (1996), *Between Here and There* (2002) and *The State of the Prisons* (2005). She is the recipient of the Patrick Kavanagh Award, the Rupert and Eithne Strong Award and the Michael Hartnett Poetry Prize and has twice been short-listed for the T.S. Eliot Prize. She is currently lecturer in creative writing at Queen's University Belfast.

PAUL MULDOON was born in 1951 in County Armagh and educated in Armagh and at Queen's University Belfast. Since 1987 he has lived in the US, where he is now Howard G.B. '21 Professor at Princeton University and Chair of the Lewis Centre for the Creative and Performing Arts. His collections of poetry include *New Weather* (1973), *Mules* (1977), *Why Brownlee Left* (1980), *Quoof* (1983), *Meeting the British* (1987), *Madoc: A Mystery* (1990), *The Annals of Chile* (1994), *Hay* (1998), *Poems 1968–1998* (2001), *Moy Sand and Gravel* (2002) and *Horse Latitudes* (2006).

FRANK ORMSBY is the author of three collections of poetry, *A Store of Candles* (1977), *Northern Spring* (1986) and *The Ghost Train* (1995) and editor of a number of anthologies including *Poets from the North of Ireland* (1979) and *The Blackbird's Nest: An Anthology of Poetry from Queen's University Belfast* (2006). He is currently working on his fourth collection of poetry.

DON PATERSON lives in Kirriemuir, Angus. His most recent collection of poems, *Landing Light*, won the T.S. Eliot Prize and the Whitbread Poetry Award. His version of Rilke's *Sonnets to Orpheus* was published by Faber in October 2006. He teaches at St Andrew's University, and is the poetry editor at Picador Macmillan.

GLENN PATTERSON was born in Belfast. He is the author of seven novels: *Burning Your Own* (1988), *Fat Lad* (1992), *Black Night at Big Thunder Mountain* (1995), *The International* (1999), *Number 5* (2003), *That Which Was* (2004) and *The Third Party* (2007). A collection of his journalistic writings, *Lapsed Protestant*, was published in 2006. He teaches creative writing at Queen's University Belfast and is a member of Aosdána.

IAN SANSOM is the current BBC writer in residence at the Seamus Heaney Centre for Poetry. He is the founder and editor of *Enthusiast, www.theenthusiast.co.uk*, and also writes for the *Guardian*. He is the author of a number of works of fiction and non-fiction. His latest book, *The Enthusiast Guide to Poetry*, will be published in November 2007.

C.K. WILLIAMS's *Collected Poems* appeared in 2006. He has published nine other books of poetry, the most recent of which, *The Singing*, won the National Book Award for 2003. His previous book, *Repair*, was awarded the 2000 Pulitzer Prize. He has published translations of Euripides' *Bacchae*, and poems of Francis Ponge, among others. He is a member of the American Academy of Arts and Letters, and teaches in the Writing Programme at Princeton University.